Psychic Detective

Keith Charles

JOHN BLAKE

First Published by John Blake Publishing, 2000

Published by John Blake Publishing Ltd,
3 Bramber Court, 2 Bramber Road,
London W14 9PB, England

ISBN 1 85782 3796

British Library Cataloguing-in-Publication Data:
A catalogue record for this book is available from
the British Library.

Typeset by Jon Davies

Printed and bound in Great Britain by
CPD, Ebbw Vale, Wales

1 3 5 7 9 10 8 6 4 2

Papers used by John Blake Publishing Ltd are natural,
recyclable products made from wood grown in sustainable
forests. The manufacturing processes conform to the
environmental regulations of the country of origin.

Contents

The Authors

Keith Charles was born in Brighton, Sussex, on 22 August 1950. He joined the police force at the age of 17. After training at the Hendon Police College he was stationed at Cannon Row Police Station in Central London, where his duties ranged from guarding the front door of 10 Downing Street to walking the Queen Mother around her beautiful garden. He has been assigned to the Fraud Squad and to the Hotel Burglary Squad. From 1992 he was working as a detective at Sutton Police Station in Surrey, until his retirement from the police force on 17 December 1999. His television appearances and tours as a clairvoyant confirm his status as one of Britain's most respected mediums.

Derek Shuff has been a journalist for more than 37 years. He was a sub-editor on the London *Evening Standard* for five years before he joined IPC Magazines as an Assistant Editor. He became a freelance showbusiness writer in 1971, and continues to contribute high-profile celebrity interviews and serialisations to national and international newspapers and magazines. He writes celebrity aitobiographies from his home near Rye in East Sussex.

Foreword

by

Jenny Seagrove

You only have to look at the night sky, brimful with stars, and wonder what is beyond 'the beyond', or contemplate infinity to know that there must be some other 'angle' on life and why we're here. I suspect we don't know the half of it. So when, in Keith's story, written simply and directly with an honesty that leaps off the page, he declares, 'this is no cranky mishap', it just reaffirmed everything that I already felt and believed.

That Keith was a policeman as well as a psychic is very reassuring. When you meet investigating officers, and I have met a few, they bring with them calm common sense, straightforwardness and the emotional detachment

v

that are absolutely vital in their job.

The common perception of a psychic tends to be of a rather vague, perhaps slightly unstable crank, whose eyes will suddenly glaze over and who starts talking or writing a lot of mumbo-jumbo. Yet how untrue this is. Every psychic I have ever met has been direct, 'together' and rather more uncomplicated than the rest of us. Only occasionally do you come across a charlatan, in it only for money and showbusiness.

If Keith was a weirdo, prone to flights of emotional fancy, I know the police force would have let him go at the start of his career, rather than see it through to his recent retirement. They even saw fit to use his gift when the occasions arose. This is a remarkable man, with a remarkable talent and a remarkable story to tell.

I have had a few psychic experiences myself. One occasion that moved me happened on television in front of about four million viewers. It was breakfast television, and sitting on the sofa with me was well-known psychic Doris Collins. My paternal grandmother had died three days before and I was wearing her wedding band on one of my fingers. All was proceeding smoothly. I had plugged the film I had been asked to talk about, and Ms Collins was in full flow. Suddenly, she paused mid-sentence, turned to me and said, 'I have a message for our young friend here.' I must confess, this was a few years ago! Then Ms

Collins proceeded to reassure me that my grandmother was all right and to tell me things only the inner circle of my family could have known. After the programme, she continued with more messages from my granny. From that moment on, I have never doubted that there is a whole new 'world' out there. I just wish I could get my phone line as clear as Keith's!

As well as being entertaining, Keith's book is reassuring. Death is no longer a dark abyss but a new horizon with something exciting beyond it that we can all look forward to journeying towards when this life ends; a kind of spiritual progress to 'the next stage', whatever that may be.

I am looking forward to my next meeting with Keith and, through him, to having a chat with my mum who has now crossed that new horizon. Who needs British Telecom?

Jenny Seagrove

Introduction

Friday, 17 December 1999 was the day I officially retired from a job that had been my life since I was seventeen, that of a London police officer. I had joined the Metropolitan Police initially as a cadet in May 1968, progressed to Hendon Police College and, after basic training, served two years in uniform before being accepted into the plain clothes Criminal Investigation Department.

Friends and police colleagues often ask me if I miss 'the Job'. I can honestly say that I don't. I have seen a great deal of life crammed into those 32 years and I have experienced many aspects of police life. I have been involved in the investigation of murders, rape, complex fraud,

Keith Charles

sexual offences against children, burglary and organised vehicle crime. It has been a part of my duty to guard royalty at Buckingham Palace, prime ministers at 10 Downing Street and Members of Parliament at Westminster. I have handled police informants and protected those individuals in fear of their lives. I have dealt with juvenile offenders through to people as notorious as Charlie Kray, but no matter what my duty has been, whether dealing with victims of crime, witnesses or offenders, I have always tried to treat each individual with consideration and respect. I am proud to say I have been Commended by the police in recognition of my detective ability and I have received letters of appreciation from members of the public and, surprisingly, letters of thanks from offenders I have arrested. Yes, I am proud to have been a policeman.

But, do I miss it? No, I don't!

There are reasons for the way I am and a part of my feelings are swayed by the fact that, for a few years prior to my retirement, many of my colleagues and I were becoming disillusioned with the police service due to the lack of recognition given to the hard work and dedication of front-line officers by senior police officers and some members of the public. I am pleased to say that these same senior officers — politicians, too — have since become aware of this failing and have now rectified the situation.

I am also very proud to say I have been a part of the best legal system and police force in the world.

There were difficulties combining my two lives, that of a police officer and a psychic medium, not least the fact that I used two names. I was born Keith William Charles Wright, but, after discovering my gifts as a medium and being invited to work in churches, I was instinctively guided by spirit to drop my surname 'Wright' when practising as a medium. There was neither deceit nor ego behind this change, and I fully advised the police in 1984 when I registered my spiritual interests. Having been named after my two grandfathers William and Charlie, it was the apparition of my 'dead' grandfather Charlie who was instrumental, I believe, in making me take on my psychic name, Keith Charles.

I was aware that not all my police colleagues shared my religious views and there was an element of jealousy from some. This was only to be expected. There were times during my career when some officers would find it good sport to poke fun at what I did. And, in return, I would have liked to have said certain things, but I bit my tongue and closed my ears to some of their personal prejudices. Really, though, it did my cause some good because even some of those bigoted officers were publicising the fact I was a medium. I am pretty thick-skinned as many police officers have learned how to be. In fact, many of my former colleagues of all ranks, from Constables to an Assistant Chief Constable, visited my public shows. Some, no doubt, out of curiosity; others I know shared my views.

I have suffered personal tragedy, such as losing my dear son Mathew in a road traffic accident on 16 November 1994. His brother Michael, my youngest son who shares the same birthday, was living for a time with a young lady named Emma. She had a beautiful daughter, Charley, who unfortunately was lost to cancer at only two years old. I remember the night before Charley passed so well. Christine, my wife, and I, had been guests of Jenny Seagrove and Bill Kenwright at the première of their film, *Don't Go Breaking My Heart* at The Odeon, Leicester Square in London. We had been rubbing shoulders with stars such as Anthony Edwards, Susan George, Lionel Blair, Linford Christie and Arséne Wenger (manager of Arsenal Football Club), Joe Royle (manager of Manchester City), along with many others, some of whom were interested in my psychic work.

On the way home, I received a call from Michael on my mobile telephone. He was at the hospital where Charley was poorly. Christine and I diverted there to join Michael and Emma. We were allowed to creep into the ward where Charley was sleeping. I gave her a kiss and said a short prayer. Little was I to know that at 8.00pm the next evening Charley would take a turn for the worse. Not long after, I was to get the call that nobody wants. Charley had passed away. I immediately drove to the hospital from my Sussex home. As I arrived outside, I was greeted by Michael who was puffing heavily on a cigarette. I gave him a hug and he took me to a side-room where I met Emma and some of her family. Despite the terrible loss they, and Emma in particular, had suffered, she told me she had asked the nurses to delay tending to Charley until I had arrived so that I could say my own private farewell to her baby. Thank you, Emma.

It was cruel that this should happen to one so young but it is no easier to accept, or deal with, when someone more mature passes away. My brilliant sister-in-law, Sue Cooper, was also lost to cancer in August 1999. She will always be in my heart.

On 18 November 1997, I was almost knocking on Heaven's door myself. I had started work at 2.00pm in the CID office at Sutton Police Station. I was feeling really good, and that same morning I'd even been sorting out my own life assurance as I was due to move home. At 2.30pm I suffered a sudden and severe pain to my throat and to my right arm. My pals 'Parky' and Liam sat me down in a quiet office. I said, 'I am having a heart-attack.'

Parky said, 'You can't be, the pain is in the wrong arm!'

So Parky drove me to St Helier Hospital in his car. I am sure we nearly reached 30mph on several occasions. All he kept saying to me was, 'Are you all right? Do you want me to go any faster?'

Struggling into casualty, I was greeted by a nurse and found myself severely out of breath and unable to answer her questions. I was rushed to a side-room where the on-duty doctor saw me and immediately started wiring me up while the nurses ripped off my clothes. A doctor from the cardiac team was summoned and all this time I was hoping against hope I was going to be told it was indigestion or a pulled muscle. When the cardiac doctor arrived, I said, 'Is it serious?'

He said, 'Oh, yes. Very serious!'

I then started to worry and Parky said, 'Oh, f***, I am going for a fag!'

I later found out that he went and phoned Christine. I often wonder why the doctor told me my situation was serious, because if I had died, I would not have come back to haunt him.

A few days later, while recovering in intensive care, I spoke to the same doctor and thanked him. I did say to him, however, that he'd frightened the life out of me when he told me it was serious. He said, '*You* frightened the life out of *me*.'

An angiogram later showed that I had had a 70 per cent blockage to my major artery. But I would like to thank Doctor Brekker and all the staff at St Helier Hospital, in Sutton, for all their efforts. I often tell the story at my shows, and the truth is that the day after my heart-attack I was given a book on how to recover from it. I was surprised to read that advice is given on how to resume a normal sex life!

Many friends and colleagues asked me what I planned to do when I left the police. I had given the matter some thought, of course, but I did not particularly fancy going into security work as many ex-police officers tend to do, so I decided instead to concentrate on my psychic and mediumship work. It had been my intention to concentrate on my public shows, private readings, teaching seminars and lectures, but I noticed that I had been consulted by corporate companies and private individuals to adapt my psychic skills to investigate crime, so I planned to put in place a combination of the two. It seemed quite a natural progression as I have had over 30 years' experience investigating crime and 20 years in mediumship. Recently, on a visit to Canada, I was invited to address the Crime Writers' Association of Canada at the Arts and Leisure Club, in Toronto. I was presented with a book and memento by the Club president. In my book, I share my investigation skills and thoughts with you, giving an insight into Canadian, American and UK cases from children through to celebrities and to royalty.

I had great fun when I was contacted by the makers of the television series *Taggart* and was asked to be an adviser in the making of an episode which was to feature actor Larry Lamb. He was to play the part of a spiritualist medium, the main character in this particular episode. Having arranged to meet Larry, he arrived at Sutton Police Station in his shorts and T-shirt, and even so he was instantly recognisable. We went to a local café and he said he wanted to be seen as a sincere medium as far as the script would let him. It was quite strange sitting in a busy coffee lounge to hear him delivering sections of his dialogue and asking me how I would deliver this in a reading.

Larry and I met on two or three occasions, including the time he came to see me demonstrate my gifts of mediumship at The Angel Centre, in Tonbridge. Throughout these meetings, I found him to be friendly and genuine.

Other stars whose paths have crossed my own, include *Coronation Street* actor Bill Roache; comedian Richard Digence; Meg in *Neighbours*; hypnotist Paul McKenna; actress Kitty Aldridge; radio personality Derek Jamieson; athlete Linda Keogh; footballer Gary Stevens (ex-Spurs and

England); entertainer Bobby Davro; television presenter Sue Barker; international film star, Leigh Taylor-Young; and many others.

In reading my book, you may find yourself being drawn to your own conclusions. I have no problem with this because I know many of you will be drawing on, and opening up, your own spiritual and psychic abilities. Maybe you will even surprise yourself how gifted you are!

Keith Charles

•1•

A Growing Awareness

I had wanted to be a policeman from the age of 15, but long before that, throughout my early childhood and formative years, I had been conscious of having a sort of heightened awareness, enabling me at times to see or sense things that were hidden to others. There were several incidents throughout my childhood that illustrate this, and perhaps the most telling concerned my friend Bobby Shafto.

Bobby Shafto was no ordinary kid. I was about eight when I first set eyes on him outside the back door of our new home in Crawley New Town, in Sussex. He was just standing there, a fairly short, dark-haired boy, in black shorts and a creased white shirt. The most striking thing about him was his shoes. They looked a bit odd, with silver buckles on the toes. I don't really know why, I suppose it was those shoes, but the name Bobby Shafto immediately came into my mind.

'Hello,' I said, shutting our back door behind me. 'What's your name?'

'Norman,' said the kid.

'Mine's Keith,' I told him. I suggested he join me and my friends down on the rec for a game of football.

'What is football?' asked Norman.

I thought he was joking. All the kids I knew played football; everyone knew football. Norman must be pulling my leg. It crossed my mind that he might have come from abroad, from some country where they didn't play football. Maybe he'd just moved into the district. Anyway, what did it matter, Norman seemed nice enough. So he tagged along and we walked off to the recreation ground for the kick-about. First I introduced Norman to my mate Dave, who was bending down tying up his shoelaces. 'You don't mind if my friend Norman joins us, do you, Dave?'

Dave looked up. 'No, of course not. Where is he?'

'Right here ... Norman, this is Dave.'

Dave started laughing. He called out to the other two who were tapping the ball to each other in front of the goal. 'Hey, guys, come over 'ere. Keith wants you to meet his new friend. The only problem is — you can't see him!' Dave let out a silly, snorting sort of laugh. Apparently, he thought I was making fun of him. 'Pull the other one, mate,' he said, turning his back on me. I didn't get it. I could see Norman perfectly clearly standing alongside me, why couldn't the others?

When I insisted that Norman was standing beside me, Dave called over: 'You must be going nuts,' adding, 'Come on, Fatty, you're in goal.'

I was very confused. Why was I the only one who could see Norman? I just couldn't understand so I thought it best to shut up about him. Norman and I met up about four or five times over the following few weeks. He would just suddenly appear, or be waiting for me when I left my house. We'd go hopping off down the street, holding hands. It's funny how I remember so clearly holding his hand. One time when we were holding hands, I took him down the length of our garden, alongside the outside wall, but by the time we'd got to the Jennings' house in Cuckmead Crescent, I couldn't see Norman any more, although I could still feel his hand in mine. Then a bit further on he reappeared again. I cannot say this bothered me. It was just that one moment he would be there, as physical as everything else around and the next he'd become invisible, even though I could still feel his presence. I couldn't explain it, though at the same time it didn't strike me as particularly unusual. I just seemed to accept the fact that he was able to make himself invisible to my friends, and to me, when it suited him.

So little Bobby Shafto was the first spirit I ever encountered, although, at the time, I knew nothing about spirits. Norman was a spirit child but I never understood who he was or why he made himself known to me. Frankly, I've never asked spirit nor have I ever really asked myself why this happened. Perhaps it was some kind of early test in my life. Or perhaps I was in the care of spirit from birth. I don't really know.

Some slightly odd things happened when I was young which have since suggested to me that, even as a kid, I had some kind of inner awareness, a sort of sixth sense which could make its presence felt in certain situations. For example, one night I had a really vivid dream. It was the sort of dream where you actually live through every detail and when you wake up you're not quite sure which is real, the dream or seeming to be awake.

Once I'd established I had been dreaming, I could recall every detail. In my dream I was playing alongside some shops and I came across a threepenny piece and two one penny coins inside a white paper bag. A few days later, I was on my way to school when I heard the voice I'd sometimes hear in my head, saying to me, 'Stop and look down ...' There on the ground in front of me was a white paper bag and inside were a threepenny piece and two one penny coins. Fivepence wasn't a lot, but to a kid of eight it was worthwhile extra pocket money. I remember thinking that it was a bit strange that I'd dreamed of finding money in a paper bag and then came across it precisely as I had dreamed I would. I even found it a bit worrying and decided I shouldn't tell anyone, not even my mum. Besides, she'd probably only have thought the worst and confiscated the money.

Another time, on my way to play football, Norman told me I would find some money on a patch of oil on the ground where an old car had been parked. I found the spot Norman had described, grovelled around for a bit and, sure enough, unearthed a sixpence. Norman was a good kid to have around! He seemed to have my interests at heart.

Maybe this was the case on the day that a friend and I decided to take the afternoon off school, and play truant. Mickey wanted us to get our bikes and take a ride somewhere well away from the school. At first I agreed, but for some reason I had a change of heart. I felt uneasy about going on our bikes, so we walked instead. Later, we found out that about the time we would have been in the old bicycle park, a bus crashed there, trapping another of our friends. He lost a leg in the accident. Whether that was a psychic warning I picked up, I cannot honestly say, but if it was then it may well have saved me and Mickey from serious injury, or even death.

Before I started seeing Norman, the spirit boy, I began to hear voices in my head. Later I was to learn that this is how many psychic-gifted people realise they are just a bit different to others, and often, like me, they don't like to tell anyone they hear these voices for fear of being ridiculed.

My own distinctive spirit voice (just one to begin with) came to me the first time during an emergency at the old Black Rock swimming pool in Brighton. The pool was later sold and broken up to make way for the now famous Brighton Marina. Within the original swimming area, there were two pools, a big one for adults and a smaller one for the kids.

On this occasion I was taken there by my Aunt Violet, my mum's sister, to get me out of my mother's hair. Shirley Chapman, a cousin, came along, too, with her small son, Ross. I'd say there were about 1,000 people in the pool area, that sunny afternoon. We were packed in like sardines. Lots of children running here and there, chasing each other, shouting to each other. People dried themselves with large, flapping towels. Pretty girls in skimpy swimming costumes stretched out in the sun.

I was just getting my mouth round a cheese and tomato sandwich after a swim, when I think it was Violet who suddenly said, 'I haven't seen

Ross for a while.' Shirley, his mum, jumped up and began looking in the direction of nearby groups, trying to spot Ross playing with other children, but he wasn't anywhere to be seen. Panic quickly took hold of both adults. Nobody had to say anything, their body language told it all. They each flew off in different directions around the two pools, while I carried on with my sandwich, not quite sure what all the fuss was about and believing that Ross would soon be found with a new friend.

It was at this point that a voice in my head began saying to me, 'He is over there.' Where? There is no way of telling precisely where, when the voice is coming from within one's head. For some reason, I instinctively looked across at a boy and girl playing in the paddling pool — along with about 80 other children.

'I can't see him,' I told the voice.

It came back again more insistently, 'He is over there.'

I got up and moved towards the young boy and girl in the paddling pool. Sure enough, there was Ross lying on his back just under the surface, unnoticed by anyone. I plucked him out of the water, put him over my shoulder and carried his limp body back to his mum. He coughed and spluttered for a bit as his mother slapped him on his back to help him clear his lungs. Within a few minutes, he was virtually back to normal, though still a little shaken by the experience. Ross was a very lucky little boy.

That incident gave me a lot to think about. I couldn't explain the voice, and I even wondered if I had been talking to myself. But I ruled this out because the voice wasn't mine. It was too grown up, much more authoritative than a small boy's voice. I also knew it wasn't someone standing behind me telling me to go and look in the pool. Frankly, at that time I could not find an explanation for the voice. I had no knowledge then of spirit voices, and it was many years later before I had them explained to me. In fact, it was a good while after I'd joined the police force, when I began taking spiritual development classes, that I was given the meaning of the voice. I was told it was psychic and that the incident with Ross was my first psychic experience. Ironically, Ross went on to become a real water baby, a Sussex county swimmer.

I am often asked to describe the voices I hear, and it is difficult to do so with any real meaning to those who don't hear them. That first voice, by the pool, was like the voice of a strict school teacher in that it was not to be ignored. It had great presence. For example, if you say to a child, 'Go over there,' nine times out of ten he or she will go without question. But if you say, 'Will you please go over there?' the same child might ask,

'Why?' The voice I heard had an urgency about it. I didn't question what it wanted me to do. It was a calm, but direct, instruction — not a request. I carried it out without question.

Poor little Ross. There he was lying in about one foot of water, drowning, and nobody had even noticed him. I knew what it was like almost to drown because it was a fate I nearly suffered on two occasions. The first was when I was about seven, at a Butlin's holiday camp.

I had got out of my depth in the camp pool and I couldn't swim. I was splashing furiously trying to keep my head above the water, with my parents and relatives watching me from the poolside, believing I was having the time of my life. That was until I slipped under a couple of times and only then realised I was in difficulty. They began arguing about who should jump in and rescue me. Apparently, my mother said she couldn't because she was wearing her new shoes, which left my dad to do the honours. He wasn't too pleased.

I was 14 when I had my next brush with death by drowning. This time my mum and dad had taken me to Arundel, in Sussex, along with a French student who was staying with us at the time. Mum was getting some ice creams. A small rubber ring we'd been playing with in the shallow end was drifting towards the deep end so I tried to grab it, but I missed. I tried again, and missed again but by now my feet couldn't touch the bottom which left me splashing and gurgling, lashing out for the ring which was just out of reach. People began shouting, 'That boy's drowning ...' and I think they were probably right. Dad could see I was out of my depth but he desperately urged me to strike out for the pool side and made it quite obvious that he had no intention of making a hero of himself a second time round. Finally, he realised he had no alternative. Fully dressed, he jumped into the water and hauled me out by the scruff of my neck. My mother came back and told my father, 'Someone in the queue said a man had to jump into the pool fully dressed to rescue a drowning boy.' Seeing him still dripping wet, she chuckled, 'Surely it wasn't you?' and added, 'Not Keith again!'

My father, Dennis John Wright, and my mother, Olive May Chapman, before she became Mrs Wright, were both very much a part of the Brighton scene. Dad was initially a lorry driver in his father's haulage business and my mum's family business was fruit and greengrocery shops. Each family employed its children, making them very family-orientated businesses. In those early days, Brighton was a close-knit community, with everyone knowing everyone else, especially if you were a Wright or a Chapman. Sometimes, the fact that I was a Wright and a Chapman was a big hindrance because I couldn't do a thing without someone knowing my mum and dad and telling on me if I stepped out of line.

I was born on 22 August 1950 in 32 West Drive, Brighton, with its 300ft-long garden, a greenhouse and a large pond, with some 300 chickens which my grandfather kept there. It was a smashing place. The house, which belonged to my grandfather, was reduced to rubble years ago to make way for three blocks of flats.

My first real memory, though, is of my brother being born on the 26 March 1954 in my grandfather Chapman's two-bedroom flat above one of his fruit shops in Bedford Street. Of course, I wasn't allowed to be present at the actual birth. I had to wait outside the bedroom door until John made his entrance into this world, then the door was opened and I was ushered in. There he was, cradled in my mum's arms for me to inspect closely. Nurse Greenhill, the midwife, looked on proudly at the result of another of her successful deliveries! Up to the age of 15, John was often called Johnny Pedlar, the nickname given to him by Nurse Greenhill. Later, I learned that 'Pedlar' was another name for 'Chapman'.

My Aunt Violet, who had her own greengrocery shop in the town, married a wrestler named Johnny Peters. Uncle Johnny and many of his wrestler friends used to come to parties laid on by my grandmother. Wrestlers such as Joe

Cornelius, Jackie Pallo, Mick McManus and Georgie Kidd were always around. To a boy, these were real heroes.

As scarce as money was, our families made sure they enjoyed themselves using any excuse to have a big party. My dad and his brothers had their own skiffle group so they soon had their parties rocking along in great style. One of Dad's musical instruments looked like a broomstick attached to a tea chest and he plucked away at the wires as you would a double bass. Obviously, he felt he could do better because he eventually bought a second-hand real double bass for a tenner. The Wright Charlies, as they called themselves at local pub gigs, became quite a legend around Brighton town.

We moved from Brighton to Crawley New Town so that Dad could take up a new job as a bread salesman with Lyon's Bakery. I went to Gossops Green Primary School and so did my mum, only she went back to school to work in the canteen to serve lunches. She had a most distinctive laugh and I could often hear it above the singing in morning assembly.

My parents never rammed religion down my throat so my belief in God, Heaven and a spiritual life after our physical death on earth came about during my development as a medium. I also believe that my life has been overseen by spirit since my birth, as it is with many people.

It's just that developing this affinity with spirit is something relatively few people choose to do or, perhaps, are aware they can do. My life and my work as a medium are in the hands of my spirit guides, my 'helpers' as we call them. To others they are their 'guardian angels'. Every medium has what is called a 'doorkeeper' whose job it is to allow spirits to make contact. My guardian angel protects me from mischievous spirits.

One of my helpers is named Kurinda, a Mongolian warrior, and he is very much a warrior. I don't see him very often, but when I do he is always waving a big sword. Then there is Charlie, a former London barrow boy who died of tuberculosis in 1605. Another, Tobias, is a young lad who was placed in a Spanish monastery when he was only 15 because his parents couldn't afford to keep him. He is very holy, very spiritual. I see him as a young man of about 25. My helper Painted Horse is an Indian healing man; a big, strong character. In fact, I call him 'Runway' because when I first became a spiritualist and linked with Painted Horse, I asked him why spirits need mediums to say what they have to say. He told me, 'We are like an aeroplane which needs a runway on which to land.' When I asked his name, he wanted to know why we on earth always want a name. He said it wasn't important and told me to call him 'Runway'. The name stuck. Only later did he tell me that his real name was Painted

Horse. Then I have a Chinese helper who is like a teacher. I don't see him often but sometimes people can see him alongside me. I don't even know his name, nor do I know the name of my little blonde helper, though she is very pretty and very cheeky. Mostly, in classes or at demonstrations, I see either Tobias, the little blonde girl or Charlie. If I see Charlie I know there is going to be a lot of good humour during the meeting. If Tobias or the Chinaman are there, then the evening tends to be a little sombre and emotional — but certainly not predictable!

·2·

Protection and Detection

My life as a police officer was never short of interest and excitement. I helped protect the Queen at Buckingham Palace, Prime Minister Edward Heath when he was at his official residence 10 Downing Street, the Queen Mother at Clarence House, Princess Anne and Mark Phillips when they were married at Westminster Abbey, as well as many diplomats, helping to ensure their safety in the sanctuary of their London embassies.

I remember Princess Anne's wedding very well. I was on duty for this State occasion as a detective in plain clothes. Along with several other CID officers, we had been *in situ* at the abbey for a few hours before the wedding was to take place. I had been involved in searching the abbey for any suspicious packages, checked the press stands, surrounding areas, the temporary scaffolding and local streets. I was to be positioned near to the entrance to the cloisters prior to the arrival of Princess Anne's State carriage.

With my colleague, we were carefully scrutinising the crowd which was growing all the time and was made up of people of all ages and nationalities. As soon as Princess Anne's carriage came into view, my senses heightened automatically. The carriage was about to draw to a halt when a tall, elderly man stepped out into its path. My colleague and I pushed through the crowd and pulled the man back on to the pavement.

'What do you think you are doing?' I shouted at him.

'Going to get my pension before the post office shuts,' he said.

I snapped back, 'It's Princess Anne's wedding. You can't go across there.'

He was particularly put out and said, 'I don't bloody care about the wedding, I've got to get my pension!'

In some cases I was on duty at these places with a loaded handgun concealed inside my tunic, the weapon discreetly hidden from public view. Sometimes, these patrols were quite scary, though not necessarily for the reasons you might imagine.

Buckingham Palace had its own regular police officers but when one went sick or was away on leave I would get called in for duty in the palace grounds. There was a small lodge within the grounds that we used for our breaks. On one such cold winter night, although I knew it was a bit irregular, I was sitting in this lodge warming my hands and feet on a one-bar electric fire and, between patrols, reading snatches of a horror book I'd brought along to help pass the time. It was about the closest we could get to any kind of home comfort.

As close as I was to this heating, my hands were still blue with the cold and my feet surely close to getting frostbite. Through the open door of the lodge I could hear the leaves on the trees and bushes rustling menacingly, shaken by an arctic blast that was sweeping across London. Shafts of bright moonlight flickered through the trees from behind fast-moving clouds. It was chillingly creepy, and I suppose my spine-tingling book didn't help the situation.

Then I began hearing things, or I thought I did, though when this happens to me I can never be quite sure if it is my psychic perception at work. Had I picked up the vibes of an intruder within the grounds of Buckingham Palace? Although it was very rare for someone to break in, it had happened before and I could quite definitely hear rustling noises from nearby bushes. This was for real and not the wind playing tricks on my imagination. As the disturbance in the bushes came closer, I could feel the hair on the back of my neck prickle in anticipation, half expecting some kind of apparition to come leaping out at me. I was only a young, quite inexperienced police constable at the time, but an enthusiastic one, so I went to face whatever it was moving around in those bushes. Gripping the handle of my truncheon, I moved in the direction of the rustling noises. I'd taken no more than three paces when all hell was let loose. The bushes in front of me parted and this 'thing' leaped out. It was a big, black Labrador on patrol with its police handler.

I could feel my heart pounding at the shock of being on the receiving end of such a surprise, though the Labrador seemed pleased to see me. Its tail was wagging like a demented metronome! As I recovered my breath and my voice, I told the handler that he'd scared the hell out of me. He just said his dog was simply being friendly, that it knew I wasn't an intruder.

Being a young copper, just up from Brighton, it gave me quite a kick to be on duty at the palace. This was the Queen's home, probably the best-known home in the world and here I was, coming from a humble, middle-class grocer's family, on duty protecting Britain's most important lady. At first it was all a bit unreal.

The Buckingham Palace garden parties were quite something for me; I loved them even though I was working. All the Lords and Ladies, the rich in their flash cars, the posers in their fine clothes and yet what amused me more than anything was that no matter who they were, on whatever level of society, they all had to queue up with their tickets to get in. It was a great leveller. I couldn't help thinking they were really no different from a crowd of football supporters waiting for the big match, but with the slightly less chance of hooliganism breaking out when the gates were finally opened.

One such garden party day was warm and sunny, with a strong westerly wind blowing. As I stood on duty at the front entrance to the palace I could see the ladies in their light summer dresses having some difficulty keeping their fancy hats on their heads. One woman lost the battle altogether as a gust of wind snatched her hat and sent it skimming across the palace forecourt like a frisbee. It landed at my feet and I instinctively stamped my foot down on its rim to stop it from being blown away again. At the same time, I couldn't bend down to pick it up because my hands were occupied trying to hold back a crowd of sightseers. Before I could do anything to help the lady in distress, a royal car drove by — right over the hat. The whole thing was a millinery disaster. The white-ribboned, broad-brimmed titfer was now flattened and dirtied beyond repair, and certainly beyond being worn in front of the Queen. The look on its owner's face as she lifted the tatty bit of cloth from the road, the contemptuous glare she gave me, is forever etched on my mind. The mishap was simply unfortunate and I felt very sorry for this guest. I could even understand that she was very angry and very embarrassed that one gust of wind had made such a spectacle of her in front of so many people, but I didn't think it was fair that she was disgusted with me because I was unable to help.

When the garden party was over and the guests were drifting away, I was standing at the main gates to the palace directing traffic out into The Mall, at the end of which, just outside the palace, is the familiar 'wedding cake' roundabout. Suddenly I was aware of a loud screeching of tyres and I looked across to the direction of the eastbound lane of The Mall, by the entrance to the park. I saw a woman being knocked into the air and landing across the bonnet of a silver Rolls Royce. With my colleague Bob, we ran across to the scene of the accident. I tended to the injured woman while Bob spoke to the driver. The woman was English (this helped because millions of foreign tourists flock to see Buckingham Palace each year), and she was aged about 60. Although she was on her back, thankfully she was conscious and had no visible injuries, except one. The front tooth of her upper jaw had virtually been knocked out and was hanging by a thread. As I spoke to her, she put her finger to the tooth, placing it between the tooth and gum socket. Now, unfortunately, I have seen many awful and gruesome sights in my time, but this simple action nearly made me throw up. I still feel queasy when I remember it. An ambulance was called and the lady was taken to Charing Cross Hospital. I am glad to say that after a check-up she was released from hospital otherwise uninjured.

When I was stationed at Cannon Row Police Station, one of my favourite duties was on Horse Guards Parade, at the back of 10 Downing Street. I just loved the Trooping of the Colour rehearsals and the sound of the pipes and drums that echoed across the parade ground. At 6.00am, with the mist swirling in off St James's Park and the haunting sound of the pipes filling the air, I found it completely spiritual. The experience sent tingles of excitement down my spine and I'd just stand there soaking it up.

The Queen Mother has always been my favourite royal so when I first met her it was all the more special for me. I was on duty at Westminster Abbey, as one of a number of police cadets forming a guard of honour. The Queen Mum came out of the abbey and when she passed in front of us we all stamped to attention and saluted, but then she suddenly stopped and began speaking to some clergymen. We had expected her to walk right past and down the path to her car. We didn't know what to do, whether to hold our salute, or drop it. The cadet next to me hissed, 'What do we do?'

I told him, 'Hold it,' which we did. Then the Queen Mother moved on and, as she passed, she turned to me and said gently, 'Thank you for waiting, officer.' I felt 10ft tall.

I was to meet the Queen Mother again, only this time inside the grounds of Clarence House, her official residence. We had a small police post in the grounds and on this particular occasion I was on duty inside the hut enjoying a cup of steaming hot tea. Suddenly, the door was pushed open and in walked the Queen Mother. I'd have been embarrassed if my own mother had walked in unannounced and caught me having a cup of tea while I was on duty, so you can imagine how I felt with the Queen Mother herself standing patiently in front of me, smiling kindly. I jumped up, stamped my feet to attention and snapped out, 'All correct, Ma'am.'

She just melted me with her smile and her loveliness, hypnotising me with her charm. 'I wondered if you might like to accompany me on a walk round the garden?' she asked.

Well, how could I refuse such a request? So off

we went. She led the way, and I tried to keep a respectful pace behind her as we slowly made our way along the garden paths. It was wonderful and I kept thinking to myself that none of my family or friends would believe what I was doing even if I had told them. I didn't say much but just answered when she spoke to me. As I say, out of respect and politeness, I walked just slightly behind the Queen Mother, although I had the impression she would have preferred me to walk more alongside her to make it easier for her to comment on the flowers that pleased her so much. After about 15 minutes I was back at my post, hardly able to believe what had just happened.

Colleagues later told me that the Queen Mother often popped in to see her Clarence House police officers, just to say 'Hello' and, occasionally, to even join them for a cup of tea, so I need not have worried that I thought she'd caught me out. I pick up auras and I was very aware of the warm aura that surrounds the Queen Mother. This showed strength, loyalty and considerable stubbornness, so not a lady to argue with because you would be unlikely to win. Having said that, I felt very comfortable in her presence. A memory to treasure.

In our police training we had never been told how to behave in the presence of royalty, so on my garden walk with the Queen Mother I simply tried to be my usual self, though I did cut the chat because I am seldom lost for words. With royalty in general, I'd always worked on the principle of not speaking unless spoken to. It was the best way of keeping out of trouble.

You will always see a police officer standing outside 10 Downing Street. Well, I have done that, too, and it can get very boring. I was there when Downing Street was open to the public and it was a favourite place with the tourists. I wonder how many of them had met the mass murderer Dennis Nilsen, now serving a life sentence in prison for killing 15 men. As a former policeman, Nilsen once did the same job as me outside Number 10 and at around the same time. Makes you think just who you might rub shoulders with!

One little old lady who called us 'my boys' came to see us every day outside Number 10. She'd walk up, say 'Hello' and give us sweets. A real diamond that one.

It was on one winter's day that I and another policeman were on duty outside the PM's pad and we agreed we needed something to stimulate our circulation. It was snowing quite hard so an impromptu snowball fight seemed to be the answer. He scooped up some of the wet snow off the pavement, pressed it into a ball and hurled it at me as though he was bowling for England. The snowball clipped my nose. Nobody was around at the time, so I bent down, scooped up my own handful of snow, pressed it into shape and hurled one back. It splattered across his chest. In no time at all, snowballs were flying in all directions, but unfortunately one of mine wasn't very well aimed, nor was it as soft as it should have been. Unknown to me, I'd scooped up a fair-sized stone with the snow because when I threw it and my mate ducked, my snowball struck one of the 10 Downing Street front windows and cracked the glass. The window didn't smash, but the pane of glass was quite badly cracked down one side. Luckily, the PM who was inside Number 10 didn't appear to hear a thing, or if he did he chose not to come to a window to find out what was going on. We two police officers decided that discretion was the better part of valour and kept the mishap to ourselves. I suppose a workman doing routine maintenance eventually found the cracked window and replaced the pane of glass.

So much for a bit of fun that went a little wrong. There were other times when the victims of our fun were the tourists. They would come up to me and say, 'Gee, is this where your Prime Minister lives?' When I said 'Yes', they would sometimes ask, 'Is it real?'

If I felt a bit bored and a tiny bit mischievous, I might go on to say, 'No, in fact what they have done here is build a false frontage,' pointing out that this was the reason there were only three house numbers — 10, 11 and 12. I would add, 'I expect when you saw Downing Street on your televisions in America you thought this was a big street? Well, as you can see, it is only a replica.'

I would continue kidding them that there was nothing behind the false frontage other than scaffolding, and explain that the Prime Minister really lived outside London in the country. They'd believe it all. Most of the coppers there played the same game because it was the best way to pass the time on duty. Sometimes we'd take it to extremes just to see how much rubbish tourists would actually believe. When asked if I was armed, I'd say, 'We are trained to kill at 30 yards — with our truncheons!'

I especially enjoyed taking the mickey out of the Americans. They would tend to ask the way to a destination in town in an antagonistic way. They wouldn't ask, 'Can you please tell me how to get to Piccadilly?' It would come out as 'Piccadilly?'

I was on duty one night in Whitehall with a fellow police officer named Steve. An American tourist really did come up to us and, looking at Steve, said, 'Piccadilly?'

Steve answered, 'Oxford Street.'

The American repeated, 'Piccadilly?'

Steve said, 'Regent Street.'

It was as much as I could do to keep a straight face as the American became more and more frustrated by Steve's reaction.

'Hey, Mac, just tell me how to get to Piccadilly, will yer?' pleaded the American.

'How did you know my name was Mac?' asked Steve.

'I guessed,' quipped the American.

'Well, guess your way to Piccadilly,' snapped Steve, as we continued on our way.

I don't want to give the impression that, as policemen, we were contemptuous of tourists. Not a bit. I liked the different people and their varying cultures. We just enjoyed stringing them along a bit, making our own lies bigger and bigger until they realised that we were kidding. It was a laugh, a harmless bit of fun, and most of them took it that way. They enjoyed chatting to British policemen. The fact that we might be armed intrigued them, too.

I joined the police force in 1969 and when I walked into the canteen at Cannon Row Police Station I would see many coppers walking around carrying handguns. It was quite frightening at first, but by the time I was doing a stint at 10 Downing Street I was also armed. I had to go on a gun training course and learn to shoot standing up and lying down. My Walther PPK, complete with a magazine primed with seven bullets, slipped into a holster under my jacket. I never used my gun, although I did have to take it out on several occasions when hunting armed suspects. Things are quite different now and the weapons training is much more thorough.

I left school in 1966 and joined the police cadets in May 1968, having had three jobs in the intervening two years. I worked for my aunt and uncle in their Brighton fruit shop, as an orders clerk in a local printer's, and I had another job as a roofing estimator. But I'd set my heart on becoming a copper, so when I was accepted to Hendon's police cadet training school for six months I couldn't have been happier. However, this happiness was a bit short-lived because at Hendon they really gave us cadets a tough time — lots of discipline, 20-mile runs, night treks, the lot. As I say, it was tough but I still enjoyed the challenge.

After Hendon I was sent as a qualified police cadet to Sunbury-on-Thames to experience day-to-day life in a police station. From there I travelled to Southall Police Station. As a cadet, I didn't have a warrant card, just a piece of blue paper authorising me to undertake school crossing patrols. It was embarrassing standing there with a lollipop sign in my hand stopping cars and waving kids across the road. All the roughnecks had a field day, wolf whistling and generally taking the mickey out of me. Being a lollipop police cadet bruised my ego a little, a bit like being a mounted policeman with only a donkey to ride!

It was around this time in my police career

that my cadet friend Kevin Kerman broke his neck. One moment he was a hero having rescued a drowning girl from the swirling waters of the Thames, the next he fell off a roof beam during training with tragic consequences. Kevin was a basketball player, a great sportsman and a good-looking boy who suddenly sustained injuries that left him paralysed from the neck down. He went straight to Stoke Mandeville Hospital where I visited him regularly, though we have lost touch since. I'd like him to know that I still think of him.

I believe I was a compassionate policeman, or I always tried to be. I was a CID officer at Paddington Police Station the day a young man was arrested for stealing a car. He was about 25 and asthmatic. Members of my own family suffered from asthma so I knew it needed to be taken seriously. An enthusiastic young police constable, with only about 12 months' service, had taken this young offender out of his cell to try and give him some air while he waited for an ambulance. I happened to be dealing with another prisoner at the time, but I took the young asthmatic a cup of tea because I could see he was in a bad way, breathing heavily and with considerable difficulty. I could also see he needed urgent assistance so I told him I'd boil some water; he could sit over it and breathe in the steam to give him some relief.

'You can't do that. He is my responsibility,' snapped the young PC. I told him I would accept responsibility and moved the prisoner across to the steaming kettle, where I began rubbing his back while he breathed in the hot vapour. Then he went off to hospital in the ambulance and I forgot all about the incident. Some time later, the handcuffed lad came back from hospital and I heard him say to his escorting officer, ''Scuse me, before you put me into a cell, I'd like to have a quick word with that officer over there,' pointing to me. He came over and said he just wanted to shake my hand for the help I'd given him. I really appreciated that little gesture.

I did my stint in uniform but I knew I really wanted to join the CID (Criminal Investigations Department). I enjoyed working with criminals because it was much more interesting than the prospect of spending the rest of my life reporting missing tax discs, defective tyres and traffic offences. Nor did I want to spend the rest of my life standing outside the front door of Number 10. Having said that, I have the utmost respect for the 'thin blue line', the front-line officers who are first to respond to emergency calls and who risk their lives daily.

When all the workers are in bed, London is a different place, even quite pleasant. I enjoyed my night duties. It was also a time when the unexpected often happened. Imagine, if you will, two uniformed coppers, hands behind their backs, in step, slowly walking along Whitehall at 0530, returning to the Cannon Row nick for breakfast. One was PC Keith Wright (that's me — Keith Charles is my clairvoyant name); the other was PC Paul Garforth. We were quite alone ... no traffic, no people, not a movement anywhere, with the exception of one solitary pigeon waddling across the road just ahead of us.

'That stupid pigeon is going to get run over,' I told Paul.

'Don't be bloody silly — pigeons don't get run over, they fly off!' said Paul in his broad Yorkshire accent.

No sooner had the words left his mouth when a taxi came from a side turning into Whitehall slap into the poor old pigeon. But it wasn't killed outright. It just lay there in the road, flapping its wings. Now I hate birds at the best of times, and this one fluttering its wings in the gutter, very close to death, disturbed me enormously. I told Paul that one of us would have to put it out of its misery, and it wasn't going to be me. He said it wasn't going to be him either.

Another copper named John was on duty near Admiralty Arch so we asked him if he would take a look at the pigeon and, if needs be, put it out of its misery.

'Not me, mate,' he told us.

So there we were, three uniformed police

officers in Whitehall bending over a half-dead pigeon and arguing over who was going to have the courage to finish it off. In the end, Paul agreed to do it. He told me to hold the bird and he would crack it across the head with his truncheon. I insisted that John held the poor pigeon, but he wouldn't so I had to do it. Gripping the poor creature at arm's length, while Paul took aim, I turned my head away and waited for the lethal blow. Paul missed.

'For Heaven's sake, wring its neck,' I told Paul, but he wouldn't. By this time, I was feeling quite ill and let go of the wretched bird, which fell on to the pavement. In desperation, Paul lashed out again with his truncheon. Again he missed the pigeon but he struck the pavement such a heavy blow that it split his truncheon in half. Now Paul would have to explain to his station Sergeant how he broke his truncheon trying to finish off a dying pigeon in Whitehall.

A couple of days later, the station Sergeant asked me if I'd seen the report from his new officer, and the wonderful story he'd produced to explain how he broke his truncheon. I told him it was true, and that I had been there when it happened. Even our hardened Sergeant had to chuckle, but said he couldn't possibly file the report because it was so unbelievable it would get him the sack. We never lived down that incident and it was the talk of Cannon Row Police Station for months. As for the injured pigeon, it was all too much for it. By the time we'd organised ourselves, it had died without our help.

As I was writing this book, my mum gave me some old photos and papers of mine which she'd kept, and among them was the following piece which I had written for my old school magazine. It was a day in my life as a uniformed bobby when I was only 19, stationed at Cannon Row after only about six months' police service.

Brrrng ... Five o'clock, time to get up. As I draw back the curtains and look out of my window, I can see the sun beginning to rise behind Big Ben, giving a touch of splendour to the 'Old Man'. I crawl out of bed and wash briskly. I reach for my trousers and they drop on the floor — never mind, I mustn't be late. I put on the usual blue shirt and button up my blue jacket. A quick brush down, on with my boots and off to work. I walk into the nick and line up in the parade room. I wonder what I shall be doing today.
'Wright?'
'Yes, Sergeant.' At least he knows I am here.
'Sixteen patrol, Wright'
'Yes, Sergeant.'
Big Ben is striking six o'clock as I walk out into Whitehall.

'Hello, mate,' says Tom the paper seller. Been there for years; happy old soul. Where shall I go? I walk up to Trafalgar Square. It's quiet at this time of morning. Only deliveries and early morning workers starting out on the same routine to do the same job day in, day out. That's one thing about this job, you never know what is going to happen.

Hello, what is that in the shop doorway? Only a pile of rags. Hang on, they moved. 'Oi, come on out of there ...' It's only one of the vagrants been having a sleep there all night. Sometimes I feel sorry for them, but in this job it doesn't pay to let your feelings get the better of you.

'Excuse me, officer. What bus do I get to the City?'

'Number 11, madam, across the road.'

'Thank you.'

Another satisfied customer.

As I step on to Trafalgar Square, I see the pigeons beginning to wake up, scattering here and there as they go off searching for food. I think I will watch the traffic for a bit. Mmmm ... that tyre is near the mark. It could cause an accident in wet weather. After watching the traffic and giving a few polite warnings, it is now half-past eight and time for breakfast.

Ah, that's better. I feel much more refreshed. A stroll round by Westminster Abbey to walk off my breakfast. One of the richest abbeys in the world, just across the road from the Houses of Parliament where all matters of importance to the country are discussed. Did you know there are just as many policemen in there as there are at my station?

Eleven o'clock, time for the guard change at Buck Palace. When I arrive there are already tourists spying upon the house of our Queen. How unsatisfactory. Fancy having about five thousand people standing in your front garden every morning. That's what it is, you know. Her grounds don't end at the railings. All the ground up as far as, and including, St James's Park, is officially part of her front garden. There are people here from all over the world — France, Japan, America, Australia ... you name it and they are here, I promise you. Thousands of them, cameras flashing and tongues wagging in every language. Still, if they can't speak English they've had it. I certainly can't speak Chinese or Russian. A bit of broken French and that's my lot.

The guards look smart. Red jackets, silver buttons, stripes in their trousers. You can see your face in their boots and, of course, the familiar busbies. Eleven-thirty and the band is here. About twenty coppers on foot and four on horses are trying to keep about five thousand people out of the way so the soldiers can get in *the palace. What fun it would be if we didn't bother and let the soldiers march in on their own. They would do it all right, no fear of that. I certainly would not stand in their way, especially with their rifles. I don't think anyone would get shot, but a few toes would get crunched.*

'Mister, I'm lost,' says a little sobbing voice behind me, and a tugging on my jacket turns me around to see a little boy aged about six.

'Don't worry, son. I will look after you. Let's look for your mummy.'

What chance is there, honestly? All these people and here am I like a right Charlie, holding this kiddy above everyone else to see if he can find his mum!

'Here, give him to me. It looks like you are holding a sack of potatoes,' says Jean. She's a woman police officer and a very good one, too. Teamwork, that's what counts and not all WPCs are built like Irish navvies, you know. They are good at their job, too. If you are getting a good hiding, you don't wait to see who is pulling the other fellow off, do you? You don't care if it's a PC or WPC and some women are just as good as some of us menfolk.

Well, the guard change is over and people are beginning to file away. It is nearly one and I have almost finished. A stroll around the park and then time to go home.

'Excuse me, I have just found this wallet.'
'Yes, sir.'
So I take possession of it, report it and take it into the station. A quarter to two, I'd better hurry. Crash ... Oh, dear, what's that? An accident just as I was going home. I'd better go and report it. Just as I said, you never can tell. I won't be home till late now. That's what makes this job so different to any other.

Ironically, only once have I been contacted by the spirit of a dead police officer. He was an incredibly tall bloke, even for a policeman. It happened at one of my shows and I could see him clearly, standing in front of me. He stared hard at me and, in a gruff voice, told me his name was Arthur. When I asked him to give me more details, he turned and showed me his service number on his uniform. He was hardly one of my most co-operative spirit contacts but then I suppose he thought I should have been out pounding my beat, rather than chatting to him over the psychic airwaves. On the flipside of this situation, few criminals who've passed into spirit have made my acquaintance from beyond. One, however, just a little cocky that he was now well out of reach of the law, came through to me and gave his name as Albert. He said that in his lifetime he had been a bit of a magpie and had spent quite a lot of time in what he described as 'one of Her Majesty's holiday camps'.

In 1971, after nearly two years in uniform at Cannon Row, I was accepted as a detective and received a posting to Kingston. It was there, in Wimbledon, that I met many tennis stars, as well as comedians Bobby Davro and Gary Wilmot. Perhaps, in some strange way, this was the beginning of me becoming what many people and newspapers now know me as — 'Psychic to the Stars'.

I was a policeman who became a psychic, which gave the British police force something to think about! They hadn't come across a psychic copper before and those in authority, even my mates, weren't quite sure what to make of what they saw as this strange new interest of mine when I came to register my activities as the police regulations required me to do.

The police are regularly swamped with offers of assistance from self-proclaimed psychics. Well-meaning callers they may be, but few of them are genuine clairvoyants. The police deal with these people politely, the attitude being that when, for example, a murder is being investigated, any offer of help is gratefully received and considered, whatever its source.

I retired as a police officer on 17 December 1999 after nearly 32 years' service, during which time I became well known around the world as Britain's 'Psychic Cop'. Newspapers and magazines published my story. Television film crews came from America and many other overseas countries to film me at work. I like to think it was good for the British police force as well as for the reputation, and good work, of genuine clairvoyants. I was able to bring a powerful credibility to the understanding of both.

By day I was Detective Constable Keith Wright, investigating and questioning the living in pursuit of the truth. Away from my police work, mostly during the evenings, I was Keith Charles, questioning the dead in pursuit of the truth from 'beyond'. No wonder it confused my bosses!

When I first officially reported my interest in spiritualism, my immediate guv'nor, a Chief Superintendent, called me to his office for a chat.

'Tell me what this is all about,' he said patiently.

I had no idea how my superiors would react to me revealing the fact that I was clairvoyant — probably with horror and considerable alarm, but I was wrong. I was certainly the first Metropolitan Police Officer to ask to register as a psychic, so they didn't know how to categorise me. I was a misfit. There was no category in which to slot me. Even so, it was necessary for me to register what was seen as my 'other business' because I would be receiving payment from a source other than the police. My payment only amounted to a couple of pounds travelling expenses, but as it was money received from outside the police service, it was necessary for me to declare it.

In the end, it was agreed that I should register as a medium, which was especially satisfying for me because it meant that the police now officially recognised my psychic work. My colleagues were intrigued, too. They wanted to know why I wanted to talk to the dead. What was I getting out of it? Did I really talk to the spirits? As you can imagine, many of them were quite cynical because they'd not even met a psychic before I came along, let alone been to a psychic meeting. Yet, here I was, one of their police colleagues. Many of them found it hard to take.

I didn't need to be too clever a detective to realise that stopping off at the local spiritualist church and talking to those in the spirit world was not most coppers' idea of a great evening out. I knew that my guv'nors found the fact that I did just that hard to understand, too. But to be fair, in the end they were happy for me to pursue those interests as long as it was in my own time, and away from work. I never abused this agreement. On the other hand, I was never told not to use my psychic gift in my work as a Metropolitan Police Officer and I did so many times.

I believe that being a psychic made me a better policeman and that being a policeman made me a better psychic. To have the two together made me unique — the only registered serving psychic police officer in Britain — and, at the time, probably in the world. There was one in New York, but he had retired long before my time in the force.

I was a better psychic being a policeman because my police training taught me how to question everything I was told. As a police detective, I dealt in hard facts, not hearsay. I knew how to seek out those hard facts through diligent questioning and I was not sidetracked by irrelevant detail.

When spirit comes through to me at my meetings, I ask it all the right questions to get detailed answers. At the same time, my psychic gift enabled me to bring a new dimension into my work as a detective — the dimension of clairvoyance, although spirit messages in themselves do not make acceptable police evidence. My boss would not have taken too kindly to me going to him and reporting that a certain spirit I'd contacted the night before had imparted important information to me that could not be backed up by hard evidence. No witness, no statement, no use!

On the other hand, my psychic 'eye' often led me in certain directions in my investigations. My reputation for this was known in police stations in the London area and because of my psychic demonstration tours around Britain, and the publicity this attracted, to regional crime squads, too. On numerous occasions, police colleagues asked me if I had any 'thoughts' about their specific investigations. Sometimes I was able to help, like the time a detective friend came to see me with a ring that had belonged to a murder victim. When I held this ring, in my head I kept hearing a particular name which later turned out to be the name of the main murder suspect. But my 'evidence' on its own was quite useless. It would have been more helpful if I had been able to say, 'Spirit is telling me that the man stabbed his victim with a knife and that the knife is in the toilet system of the house next door!' Bingo. The detectives recover the knife, find the fingerprints and arrest the murderer. In evidence, they would then just say that as a result of information received, they went to a certain house and found the murder weapon. This is the only way psychic information can really be used in police detection.

One especially interesting piece of psychic information which I received related to the mysterious disappearance of estate agent Suzy Lamplugh. Later in this book, I focus on some of the most mysterious deaths and disappearances of our time and use my psychic detection skills to focus on these. Suzy's still unsolved disappearance is one such case. Others include the murder of Jill Dando, the tragic death of Princess Diana, the suicide of rock star Michael Hutchence, the mysterious death of former newspaper tycoon Robert Maxwell and the mysterious disappearance of Manic Street Preacher pop star Richey Edwards.

But back to police investigations. One such case concerned a boy named Lee Boxall who went missing in Croydon, Surrey, on his way to a football match. Detectives working on that case had over 50 so-called mediums ring in with their theories. One officer at the station got in touch and told me his guv'nor wanted to see me to find out if any of these mediums were known to me. One or two of them had come up with some quite interesting information, but the police were worried that one of those ringing in could be a suspect sounding out the police to find out what they knew, or didn't know. I was able to aid the inquiry by identifying some of the mediums who wanted to help.

To give you some idea of the kind of useless information the police can be given, one well-known medium rang to say that the boy's body would be found within 50 miles of water. That was it, nothing more. You cannot go anywhere in Britain without being much more than 50 miles from water! That kind of call just wastes police time. My prayers go out to the Boxalls and all families in similar situations.

Some mediums, knowing I am a police officer as well as a medium, would ring me with their spirit messages or their dreams. Most of them meant well and passed on their information feeling that they might prevent someone from being arrested if they didn't. I always asked them in future to question the information they intended to give to the police before actually doing so. Did it answer the kind of questions a policeman would ask them? If it did, fine, ring in. If not, then save the cost of their phone call.

When I interviewed a suspect, or people connected with a crime, I would get very strong feelings as if spirit was around me, watching over me, guiding my questioning. When it made me go goosepimply, I knew I was on to something or someone. Once, when I was working on a rape case which happened at Kingston Hospital, one of the lads on the crime squad was asked by Cannon Row police to arrest a particular man for common assault. I told the arresting officer that I was looking for a rapist and made it my business to find out what kind of common assault was involved because I was getting very strong vibes this same man was the one I wanted for the hospital rape. I discovered he had tried to drag a young woman into his car. When I called at the man's home, he wasn't there but his mother was. She was a nice lady, really charming and invited me indoors. I just knew I was in the right house and that the same young man was responsible for the two offences. Spirit confirmed my feelings.

Sometimes, one of my methods of questioning was to give people the impression I had met them before, even though I knew I hadn't. This was a useful technique which enabled me to ask questions without raising suspicion and putting people on their guard. Often it was the only way to get information I desperately needed. If my casual form of questioning confirmed I was barking up the wrong tree, then no harm was done. On the other hand, if I was right ...

So I was chatting away to this lad's mum and I said to her, 'I know your boy, don't I?' I told her I thought I used to play football with him. 'He has a really hairy chest,' I said. 'He used to work at so-and-so.'

The lady was stunned. 'Well, yes, he does. How did you know that?' I knew then that spirit had put me on the right track and into the right house. The man was subsequently arrested and charged.

It is difficult for me to describe the difference between intuition and spirit help because they are both 'feelings' that enter my mind. Yet I know there is a distinct difference. So, was it psychic or was it intuition when the name Ricky came into my head during a murder inquiry in Wimbledon I was involved in?

The victim had been a taxi driver. At the station, there was a book in which we had to enter the name of any suspect we thought might be relevant. I didn't know this Ricky, whose name had just came into my head, but I did know his brother. It turned out that Ricky hadn't actually committed the taxi driver murder but when we investigated him we discovered that on the same day he had kidnapped a girl, taken her into Richmond and had killed her. A few days later, he told another girl what he had done, then killed her, too. Ricky was arrested, brought back to our station and charged, but he hanged himself in Brixton prison whilst on remand.

There was no doubt that my psychic instinct triggered me into action when a friend and I were on our way to work at Cannon Row Police Station. As we walked past Big Ben, a kid on a scooter drew up just ahead of us. For some reason, I said to my mate, 'Come on, he has nicked that scooter!'

We ran over to this bloke and I asked him where he'd got it. He threw the machine at my mate, Mickey, and ran off down the road, through the traffic lights towards the Houses of Parliament, with me hot on his heels. I caught up with him, slammed him against the waist-high wall that runs alongside the Houses of Parliament and forced his hands behind his back. In the struggle we both nearly fell over the wall into the Thames. He had stolen the scooter a few hundred yards away, outside the former Greater London Council building.

In police work you develop a sixth sense, but it has a lot to do with the way you are trained to look around you. I might be driving past a row of houses and notice someone in jeans, trainers and jogging top standing looking around them. That would draw my attention and encourage me to take a second look. It was not intuition; it was the experience you learned as a policeman. I'd look at a person's shoes, look to see if he had a mate, look to see if there was a car parked nearby. So what was he up to? As I say, this was crime detection experience. Most people would walk right past someone looking like that, and not think for one moment that he might be up to no good.

When my spiritual intuition made me aware, it was quite different. I would hear a voice in my head say, 'Look round the corner.' I'd see a man pacing up and down. I'd get little leads about things I couldn't see. Or I would be driving along a road and the same voice in my head would suddenly tell me to turn left. I'd turn left and see somebody stealing a car. Strange little things like that often happened to me.

Humour plays its part, too. I am not sure whether it was psychic feeling or straightforward human intuition that told me the reason for an elderly Hastings woman's joy when I delivered what I thought would be the shattering news that her husband had just died. I drove to the council estate where she lived, found the house and parked my police car outside. As I approached the front gate and unlatched it, I could see a woman cleaning her windows. 'Hello, love,' she called out as I walked towards her.

'Mrs Smith?' I asked.

'Yes, love. My old man, is it?'

'Well, yes. Could you come down off the chair,' I asked gently.

'Dead is he?'

'Well, yes, he is,' I told her, half expecting the poor woman to burst into floods of tears.

'OK, love. Thanks,' was all she said, and she turned round to carry on cleaning her windows.

I walked away hardly believing the conversation I'd just had. Three weeks later a letter arrived at Hastings Police Station from the window-cleaning lady, thanking the officer for the kind and considerate way he'd delivered the sad news of her husband's death. Call me a cynic, but my instinct told me the little old lady had inherited a few bob from her old man!

I was pounding my beat late one wet night during my spell in Hastings when a couple of police mates stopped by. Ian and Ginge, a woman police officer, invited me to sit in their car for a smoke. As we chatted, quite suddenly a voice in my head said, 'A stolen car is going to come by ...'

I told Ian and Ginge, 'You are going to laugh, but I can tell you that a stolen car is going to come through the traffic lights just behind us any moment.'

In fact, we sat on the Hastings seafront for another 15 minutes and not a single car passed us. Then a Morris 1100 appeared and drove straight through the amber lights. Four people were inside.

'Come on, Ian. That's the one,' I shouted.

We chased the Morris for eight miles, having been told over the radio it had been stolen in Sutton the previous night. Ian and Ginge couldn't believe it. Finally we managed to stop the car and arrest the occupants, but I didn't have the heart to tell them I knew they were coming our way. They'd never have believed it if I'd told them the spirit world had tipped me off! It was another example of how my clairvoyance played a very important part in my police work.

Early on in my police career, as I also developed my skills as a psychic, I made a point of keeping the two worlds apart. This was one of the reasons I decided to call myself Keith Charles as a psychic, so that my real name, Keith Wright, was kept for my police work and my private life. Just occasionally, however, the two did come dangerously close, because there was always the possibility that at one of my psychic meetings I would meet someone I had investigated, or even arrested, as a police officer.

Once I accompanied two colleagues with a

warrant to search a house. We ended up becoming involved in a fight with the whole family and their neighbours. It became so rough that we had to call for back-up. My friend was then hit with a shovel and a girl grabbed hold of my testicles and wouldn't let go. The whole situation became quite violent. Eventually, help arrived in the shape of one police constable on his bicycle, pedalling his heart out at what must have been all of 1.7mph. The three of us, plus PC Plod, were still no match for the dozen or more family and friends making it quite clear that our presence wasn't appreciated. Anyway, calm was eventually restored and the offenders were later dealt with in court.

Eighteen months later, I was on a spiritualist church stage giving messages when I spotted the same mum, daughter, son and one of the neighbours involved in the fracas, sitting together in the back row. I hoped they hadn't recognised me. Afterwards they came up for a chat and the mum asked me what I did for a living. I told her I worked for the government, which wasn't really a lie. The daughter said my face looked familiar — maybe we'd met before — but she didn't twig that I was the police officer she had so uncomfortably compromised at her house when I'd tried to search it. That was a real rough and tumble and I wasn't too disturbed when those particular people got their come-uppance in court. Sometimes my need to act strictly to the letter of the law as a policeman did conflict with my instinctive need as a compassionate medium to go out of my way to help people. I have to admit that finding the right balance was sometimes quite difficult.

I had to see myself as a detective whose job it was to go out and fight crime. The people I might have been arresting one moment, I could have been helping spiritually the next. I didn't necessarily know they had been in trouble with the law. Alas, criminals do not go round with 'criminal' stamped across their forehead.

When my ex-wife Maureen asked me if a friend of a friend could come to see me for a reading, I agreed but I had no idea why she wanted a reading, other than out of curiosity. As it happened, it turned out to be a very emotional experience for all of us — me, Maureen, the woman and her husband. The woman came to my home in Molesey, Surrey, and we sat in our kid's playroom where there happened to be a washing machine and a comfortable sofa. As we chatted over a cup of tea, I became aware of the presence of a young spirit girl in the room with us, who turned out to be the daughter of the couple in the kitchen with us. Through communication, I quickly established that psychically we were in Brighton. This was to do with a man named Russell Bishop who had been cleared of murdering the daughter and another young girl in the so-called 'Babes in the Woods' murders.

I could actually see the child. She was sitting on the washing machine, dangling her feet over the side and swinging a pink elephant which the little girl's mum told me had been her daughter's favourite toy. The little spirit girl wanted her mum to know that she was happy in Heaven and that her spirit was always with her mother. Personal messages were passed and it was, of course, very traumatic for the parents. Bishop was cleared of the 'Babes' murders in Moulsecoomb, in Brighton, but he was later found guilty of the attempted murder of a young girl and imprisoned.

In one murder case I was investigating I had to tell a woman that her husband had been shot dead. His name was Eddie Roberts. He was a Londoner and had been shot outside a pub in Norbury. As I pulled up outside Mrs Roberts' house, I called upon spirit to help make this easier for me. Then I spotted a car in the driveway with the registration letters KWC — my own initials — which, to me, was a great omen. I knocked on the door and told the woman the bad news. Then her son and daughter came home. In fact, the daughter, Rachel, later had one of the main parts in the children's television series *Grange Hill*. I was made family liaison officer and came to know this family very well. A couple of days after my first visit, an aunt came to the house and when she saw me sitting in the lounge, she said, 'What are you doing here?' I actually knew this woman as a spiritualist. First the initials KWC on the car, then this aunt turning out to be another spiritualist. It was as though my involvement had been predestined. The strange course of events then continued.

I had to go to Epsom on Derby Day to make further inquiries in connection with the murder of Eddie Roberts to see a possible witness I only knew as Bill. On my way to Epsom, I kept saying to spirit, 'Come on, give me the surname of this man. Bill who?' I got nothing, so I continued talking out loud to spirit. 'All right then, his name will be on the next lorry that comes along ...' A lorry came into view and as it passed I could see on the side of the vehicle the words 'Taylor's Removals'. When I reached the Epsom workplace where I believed I was going to find my witness, I asked to see Bill.

'Bill who? We've got a lot of Bills,' said the guy at reception.

'Bill Taylor,' I told him.

'Right, he's over there.'

He pointed to a man working in one corner of the building. And he was my man. Spirit had come up trumps yet again.

Sometimes my police work brought me into direct contact with celebrities. Mike Winters, of the one-time comedy duo Mike and Bernie Winters, was one such celebrity. It was a situation in which my psychic ability would succeed again. I went to a West London hotel in which Mike had been the victim of a robbery. As soon as I went into his apartment, I had very strong and specific feelings about the robbery and what had, and had not, been stolen. Almost before I had even introduced myself, Mike, who is now a full-time writer living in Miami, led me into his sitting room. I just stood there turning slowly on my heels, absorbing the vibes I could feel flowing through me.

Mike looked a bit puzzled, then asked, 'What is it?' perhaps thinking I was doing my Sherlock Holmes bit and was about to come up with some stunning solution! I don't know about stunning, but I think he was quite surprised when I explained. I told him that apart from being a copper I was also a clairvoyant and that, for some strange reason, I was picking up vibes about the robbery. He seemed especially fascinated, although I wasn't really sure why until later when he revealed that his next book was to be about a medium who solved a rape case using his psychic powers!

'So what do you feel about this one, then?' he asked, egging me on with a partly personal and partly professional interest.

'I can tell you that your wife won't be seeing

her jewellery again, apart from one very special piece,' I told him. I was right, too. That one special piece was his wife's antique gold watch which had been well out of reach when the thief paid his unwelcome visit.

'I took that piece to the jewellers to have it cleaned only this morning, before the break-in,' said Mike.

This incident, and my own involvement in it, found its way into the newspapers. Mike told one reporter, 'I became fascinated with Keith's dual life, a policeman by day and a medium by night. That is why, in my book *Razor Sharp*, I had the main character use a psychic to solve a rape case.'

I have remained friends with Mike Winters ever since. Mike recently said of me: 'I suppose I hadn't given much thought to the possibility of there being life after death, but that all changed in 1989 when I lost so many dear people, including my brother Bernie, my brother-in-law, my sister-in-law, my mother-in-law and my niece, as well as dear showbusiness friends such as Dickie Henderson and Matt Monro. These tragedies preyed on my mind so it was good to have Keith giving me some spiritual warmth and comfort. When the finality of death hits you on such a personal level, many questions tend to flood into your mind. I was no exception.

'As a writer, I am fully aware of the need to question all things around me. Keith is a new breed of psychic and being a police officer, he is skilled in asking questions. He is especially suited to the task of bringing more understanding about our fate, or rather, the fate of our souls when we have come to the end of our earthly existence. Our understanding of life, although still minimal, has probably never been greater; our understanding of the possibility of a form of life after death must be even more seriously considered. Whether you believe in life after death or not is probably academic. The fact is that until it can be finally proved, it cannot be acceptably disproved!'

Such independent views help not only me, in what is now my full-time work as a medium, but those like me all over the world who genuinely believe we have this wonderful message for everyone.

Not everyone believes it, of course, or wants to hear it. There was a time when mediums were regarded by the police generally as a nuisance and those members of the public who rang in with their psychic information were not taken too seriously. But long before I retired from the police force, that attitude changed dramatically. The police are now much more open-minded about all information given to them in good faith by mediums or anyone else. I found that over the last five or six years of my service, I was contacted by various branches of the police service from traffic patrol officers, murder squad detectives and those dealing with missing persons.

I only came across one senior police officer (now retired) who told me point-blank that my psychic gift was a load of rubbish. He was upset when he overheard me at work talking to a civilian girl typist. We were chatting about her brother-in-law, a well-known professional boxer I wanted to meet, but this particular Chief Inspector decided it was a good enough excuse for him to have a real go at me over my spiritualist beliefs.

He stormed into our office and, in front of the young typist, he accused me of discussing my psychic work with the girl, saying I was trying to turn her head. Turning her head? She was in her mid-twenties, not a young apprentice of 16. I just saw red and decided, senior officer or not, I must have it out with this man. For some reason he was clearly troubled by anything to do with the psychic world and I was just a scapegoat for this inner fear of his. He was totally out of order having a go at me, so I followed him to his office and respectfully told him he owed me an apology.

'No I don't,' he snapped back. He again repeated his accusation that I had been discussing spiritualism and that he would not tolerate me bringing my outside interests into his office. I repeated that I had not been discussing spiritualism with Elaine, but her professional boxer brother-in-law. He still wouldn't believe me so I called in Elaine and asked her to confirm this, which she did.

By this time things had begun to get a bit heavy. My guv'nor ordered us both out of his office — or he'd throw us out. Elaine left but I stayed where I was to continue to argue my point. Our raised voices, I was to learn later, were heard in the rest of the office. The next day the matter seemed to have been forgotten, or cooled down, because the guv'nor heard someone discussing the row we'd had and eavesdropped a while. I chipped in and said the row had been between me and the guv'nor, who just smiled, said 'Yes' and moved off. End of the matter. I don't think I'd have had much chance of converting my ex-guv'nor to spiritualism but I do know a good number of my former police colleagues did see my demonstrations, although there was no way I would have deliberately tried to recruit any of them into spiritualism. If they were sufficiently interested to ask me about the psychic world, then I was happy to tell them and try to answer their questions.

Policemen tend to be cynical. They want everything spelled out to them. I would hate to have to put on one of my clairvoyance demonstrations to an audience of coppers. So far this hasn't happened. Well, I wouldn't actually hate it, but I would certainly receive some stick from them. Having said that, I did offer to hold an 'Awareness Day' for my colleagues, many of whom were interested and some who came along to one of my tutorial seminars made surprisingly good students.

One thing about being a detective and a spiritualist was that each was good training for the other. As a detective, I was mostly on a hiding to nothing with the public, just as I am as a spiritualist. The general public see us both as fair game for their mickey-taking, but this never bothered me. I came to terms with this public attitude soon after I joined the force and became the butt of silly jokes. Mostly, no malice was intended, it is just the way some people handle a situation involving a police officer and in which they are not always comfortable. I found the answer was to help make them feel comfortable.

It is precisely the same with spiritualism. People take the mickey out of spiritualism, life after death and mediumship because it is not something they understand or are comfortable with. They are out of their depth, so they have to cover up their ignorance by making fun of it. Take offence, get angry and become abusive and you have shown up your vulnerability. Show them you can share their fun at your own expense, or give them an equally cheeky response and they feel comfortable with your authority or your knowledge which, at this level, exceeds theirs.

As a detective, I had considerable power of authority invested in me so that I could do my duty in the public service. As a spiritualist I am on the other side of the counter, so to speak; just another member of the public with no authority other than my ability to communicate with souls in the spirit world. In both, compassion is essential.

I never needed compassion more than I did during the Clapham train crash. I was on office duty and my station at Battersea had the task of dealing with it. Half the staff had to go to the scene of the crash. I saw the look of anguish and despair on their faces and on the faces of the other workers who spent many days in the local mortuary. I found myself very much involved with those dead victims moving on to the spirit world.

I had my lighter moments, too, though these were quite often at my expense. The telephone would ring and someone would say, 'Keith, it's for you — but then I expect you already know that!' Or a copper would tell me that clairvoyance is a load of old rubbish, then when we were alone together he'd ask if I could pick up something on him. I'd get challenged to forecast who'd win horse races, but I never played those games. In the police, I just laughed them off.

Another favourite was the play on words. They'd talk loudly among themselves, making sure I could hear, about how Keith likes medium red wine or medium dry sherry. The same old quips day after day sometimes became a bit tedious, but I always kept cool over the mickey-taking. I accepted that as a medium I was open to ribbing. Besides, in my youth I was a fat kid and learned how to handle teasing at an early age. It never bothered me.

·3·

My Way

The little girl's voice was clear. She was telling me she had died in a car crash and that she had come in spirit this particular evening to say 'thank you' to someone in the audience. I could hear her deep inside my head in the same way you might 'think' something a person is saying to you; it's probably the only way I can describe how I 'hear' spirit voices. As I received the spirit girl's words, I passed them on to a hushed audience from the stage of the Corn Exchange, in the Kent town of Maidstone.

It was a rather damp autumn evening and yet the hall was packed to capacity. People were even standing in the aisles and at the back. We were in the part of the evening where I give messages and right now my task was to try to find the right man for this little spirit child. The atmosphere was electric as I set about this task.

'His name is Dave, she is telling me,' I continued, my eyes scanning the rows of people for a raised hand or even someone just shuffling about in their seat looking very uncomfortable. When people believe a message is for them, it can come as a bit of a shock and they become nervous, reluctant to link up. 'Come on, Dave, show yourself so that I can link you to this little girl ...' Still no response. People were looking over their shoulders, hoping to see Dave identify himself because they were bursting with curiosity. They wanted to know what was behind this link to spirit, made still more interesting because a child was involved.

'He is at the back,' the spirit girl told me. I had a microphone so I knew I could be heard even at the far end of the hall, and in the audience I had a helper with a cordless microphone so that when I found Dave we would hear his responses. But where was Dave?

What I didn't know at the time was that Dave and a woman, perhaps his wife, were sitting some four rows from the back. My co-author, Derek Shuff, was accompanying me to meetings as a part of his research for this book. Unknown to me, he had positioned himself on a gallery alongside the projection room window so that he could look down from behind the audience and observe their reactions unnoticed. Long before I discovered the identity of the bashful Dave, Derek had spotted the woman next to him, apparently urging him to stand up and be identified. But he kept shaking his head, not wanting to be involved.

I related still more information as it was being passed on to me by the spirit girl, and as I did so this woman apparently became more and more frustrated that Dave would not acknowledge the message was for him. I related the information that the Dave I was looking for had just bought a car for £400, and as I did so I was drawn to a man toward the back of the hall. 'Is your name Dave?' I asked him.

He said it was.

'Have you just bought a car for £400?'

No, he had not, so he was clearly not the Dave I was after.

'How will I know I have the right Dave?' I asked the spirit child.

'He has a tattoo which shows a heart with a swallow diving through the heart,' she told me.

I passed this startling new information to the audience. At this point, the woman in the fourth row from the back almost heaved the man next to her out of his seat. He was immediately behind the other Dave I had just talked to. My helper with the microphone went straight to him.

'Yes, my name is Dave, but it is my second name. My first name is Paul,' he said nervously.

I thanked him for identifying himself and asked if he had just bought a car and did he have a tattoo on his right arm?

'I bought a car today for £400 and, yes, I do have a tattoo like you described on my right arm.'

The audience was spellbound. You could have heard a pin drop; heads were turned to the back. I was able to tell Dave that he had another tattoo on his left arm which he wanted removed because he no longer liked some words on it. He agreed this was also true.

So, I knew I had found the right Dave and it was clear to me and to the audience that this was not the kind of attention he wanted to attract. His voice was subdued, and he just couldn't understand how I seemed to know so much.

'This little girl has come back from the spirit world to thank you. Let me tell everyone how you met. She was about seven and in a car with her mother on their way home on a wet winter's evening and there was an accident. The car left the road, crashed into a tree, instantly killing the child's mother, then the vehicle caught fire. A few moments after the crash you arrived at the scene from the other direction. It was a horrifying sight, with the car starting to burn and the little girl at the window trying to get out ...'

As the spirit child continued her story through me, from the stunned look on Dave's face, I could see it was precisely as I had described it. Then tears flowed down Dave's cheeks as he relived the horror of that night.

'Without hesitation, you lifted the child from the car, cradled her in your arms and sat with her on the roadside as other motorists and the rescue services dealt with the fire and the child's mother. The little girl is telling me that as you cradled her head in your bare arms, one of her last earthly memories was your heart and swallow tattoo. Sadly for you, though, she passed into the spirit world.'

It was all too much for Dave to hear and relive. He wept quite openly, comforted by the lady with him. She was in tears, too. From the handkerchiefs which suddenly appeared in the dimly lit auditorium, it was clear that quite a few people out there were in tears. The little girl asked Dave not to be sad any longer over her death. She wanted him to know that she was happy in the spirit world with her mother, and she wanted her rescuer's earthly life to be happy, too. The audience broke into spontaneous applause at this touching link with the spirit world. This was good evidence, the kind of spirit co-operation that makes some of my meetings really buzz.

No, I cannot cajole spirit or an audience into creating the right atmosphere. Those who come to my meetings are looking for positive proof of life after death. When spirit comes to them they are satisfied beyond any shadow of doubt that the link is genuine. Neither can I force spirit to come back and communicate. People who go to my meetings attend out of curiosity because they desperately want to contact a loved one, or even just to rubbish the whole idea.

My style of mediumship is probably unique because I like to bring a sense of fun into my contact with both earthly audiences and spirit links. I want none of the mystery and mumbo-jumbo associated with traditional spiritualism, so people either like the way I talk to those who have passed on, or they don't. It either entertains them, or it offends them.

I warm up my audiences just as a comedian will warm up a television studio audience. I welcome them, tell them a few funny stories and probably even joke a bit at the expense of some of those there. If I can get them to laugh, feel relaxed and bring meaningful messages to a number of them, then they will go away after a few hours having had a wonderful evening. It whets the appetite and they will want to come back for more. The trouble is that those who come out of curiosity are often just a little bit nervous, and wonder how they will cope if they are given a message. If there are 1,000 people in an audience, the chances are that I will manage to give out only about ten messages, and these have to be good quality. So the chance of receiving a message is not necessarily particularly high at a public meeting.

I did my first public demonstration through Derek Robinson, my agent and road manager, on Friday, 9 September 1983, in Kettering. Another medium named Fred Reynolds was the star turn. How well I remember that first occasion when I went on stage. There was seating for about 500 in what I think was the town hall. There were wooden arches set into the walls and dusty paintings of cavaliers and kings looked down on us. The stage creaked as I walked across it and there was no public address system.

Not being an actor with a booming voice, and wanting to be sure my initiation went without a hitch, I had borrowed a small, portable, 40-watt amplifier with a hand-held microphone. Even though I was naturally apprehensive, I was excited. By the opening of the meeting, some 300 faces were looking up at the platform. Fred did his bit. Derek Robinson tried hard, too, to ensure there were no problems. Unfortunately, none of us had taken into account the 'walking dead' of Kettering who'd joined our audience. They seemed intrigued but showed very little reaction.

I went on at about 8.45pm my usual chirpy self, full of fun and chivvying the audience into some kind of response, even if it was 'Shut up and get off!' No such luck. I told one man he drove a white van, to which he said, 'Yes.' Then I told him he wanted to sell it, and he said, 'No.' I didn't seem to be getting anywhere. I had only been on stage 15 minutes, yet people began getting up and leaving. A trickle turned into a torrent. I felt absolutely awful and completely to blame for what appeared to me to be my total failure with my first public demonstration. All right, it had been a struggle but had I really been so bad?

When the meeting was closed, some people from the local spiritualist church told me how much they had enjoyed my demonstration of clairvoyance. I felt they were just being kind, knowing it was my first time. I told them they didn't need to show me any sympathy; I was the one who was sorry that so many people had decided to leave before I had finished.

'Oh, that was nothing to do with you,' said the secretary. 'The last bus goes at 9.10pm and those people who left early had to make sure they were on it.' I wasn't due to finish until 9.30pm and nobody had thought to tell me about the last bus!

I have discovered the hard way that clairvoyants have to be prepared for all kinds of distractions. Often I am on stage battling against people slurping beer and Coke out of cans, or trying hard to be heard over the rustling of crisps and sweet packets. The sudden flare of a match in a dimly lit hall can also be very distracting. Worst of all, though, is the small party of six or so women sitting only a few rows back from the stage, all wanting to tell each other at the same time about the dreadful day they'd just had. Try to stop an audience from drinking, munching or chatting during a show, and they let you know in no uncertain terms that anyone on stage is just a diversion when they have run out of conversation! I've been told to 'Sod off' several times for interrupting such girls' nights out.

Much of my early show experience came through Derek who worked very closely with the late Doris Stokes, and Gordon Higginson. For me, Gordon will always be the Master, one of the most gifted British mediums. Doris Stokes knew how to handle an audience probably better than anyone. Her stage presence was her strength and she knew how to get an audience eating out of her hands. She also had her enemies. One particular vicar named the Reverend Ronald Granger was positively hostile when it leaked out that Doris and I were planning a psychic meeting in his Petersfield parish. The *Sun* newspaper carried a huge headline which left Doris Stokes in no doubt that neither her physical nor spiritual presence was welcome there — MESSAGE FOR DORIS STOKES: GET LOST it screamed. The report went on to read, 'The angry warning was delivered by vicar Ronald Granger who claims the famous medium is "un-Christian". The Rev Granger doesn't believe Doris really talks to the dead and he has told councillors at Petersfield, in Hampshire, they should ban her from speaking in the town.' According to this clergyman, the New Testament teaches that people don't automatically live on after death and he believed it was very unhelpful for people to be told they did.

'One has to learn to face death. I have known of many cases where people have grieved more after going to a spiritualist,' he insisted. After this broadside from Petersfield, Doris decided to give the town a miss, adding, 'I've got no plans to visit Petersfield. Plenty of other people are only too keen to hear me.'

When the Petersfield farce reached Doris, she was quickly on the telephone to me to sound off. I was sitting at my desk in Norbury Police Station when Doris came on the line, and she was clearly in a foul mood.

'What's this nonsense you have been telling the *Sun* about me and you being banned from Petersfield?' she snapped. It was about 8.30am and Doris was in fighting form. 'I have not been banned from anywhere,' she continued.

Frankly, I didn't know what she was talking

about and I told her so.

'Go and get the paper and ring me back,' she ordered.

I bought the newspaper, rang her back and asked her what the problem was. 'So, they got it all wrong,' I told her.

'You must have given them an interview,' she retaliated, to which I said I had not. It took some 20 minutes before she finally calmed down and rang off.

Doris Stokes's ego was again dented when my name instead of hers was mentioned during a press reception that Doris had laid on on board the Orient Express. Doris had paid British Rail £100 a head for a number of reporters to be entertained on the train journey from Victoria to Hollingbourne, near Maidstone. A reporter brought up the Petersfield ban so my name became part of the discussion, but Doris was not amused because she thought I was using her name to gain publicity for myself. Backing off, as Doris did when she was confronted by a disbeliever such as Ronald Granger, was just about the worst thing she could have done.

In the psychic world, we all owe a great deal to Doris Stokes because she did more than most in the years up to her death to draw attention to spiritualism. Another Doris — Doris Collins — had hoped to take over her namesake's mantle, but this never happened. They were often confused and this irritated Doris Collins, but even with Doris Stokes in her grave, Doris Collins remained very much in the other Doris's shadow.

There will never be another Doris Stokes. She quickly warmed to this direct contact with people and because of her personality they quickly warmed to her. They loved the bedside manner which she cultivated so expertly, the 'Hello, lovey. I have your dad with me ...' approach to putting the living in touch with the dead. She quickly became everybody's lovable grandmother of mediumship and they trusted her. It was a winning formula.

Doris Stokes appeared at The Palladium, in London, and the meeting sold out faster than an appearance by The Beatles. At Lewisham Town Hall, it was advertised that tickets to the Doris Stokes demonstration would go on sale at 9.00am, but the staff were there at 6.30am selling tea and sandwiches to the huge queue of followers who had started arriving much earlier.

But this cult following for Doris Stokes was not to last. After a while she began to attract some hostility. Newspapers began to take a long, hard look at the businesslike woman behind the lovable little old lady image. In her heyday, she was attracting capacity audiences up to 5,000 strong. This put her under tremendous pressure to come up with good spirit links.

I know from personal experience that clairvoyance is never easy. It is hard work and, for various reasons, some evenings can go better than others. I am sure some people believe you have a direct line that mediums magically switch on when they stand on stage. I know that some of my stage performances will be better than others; there are many factors which influence this. These range from the alertness and willingness of the audience to respond and participate, to the general wellbeing and health of the medium (I once did a show seven days after being released from hospital) and other background factors. It is a no-win situation for us mediums. I don't mind criticism provided it is constructive. Even my close friends, who hold differing views on what I do, grill me when I am out socially. It was even suggested that prior to a show, I research members of the audience. I would be amazingly clairvoyant to know in advance who was going to come to my shows!

Doris Stokes was probably an ordinary medium, but she was an extraordinary woman. I take my hat off to her memory for bringing spiritualism out of the closet and on behalf of the enormous number of people who benefited from her charitable work. I learned a lot from her, just watching her stage performances. Derek would say to me, 'See how Doris does it,' in terms of how she would stand on a stage, sit on it, or just move around it.

On our way by car to meetings all round Britain he would often test me, asking if I could pick up spirit messages as we were driving along. Sometimes I could, sometimes not. However, we both knew I wasn't another Doris Stokes or another Gordon Higginson in terms of my style of presentation. I was a one-off, cheeky clairvoyant and from the very start I wanted to break all the rules of linking with the spirit world. I wanted to do it my way.

I don't want my shows to be a morbid, mystical, scary experience. I want them to be fun, bubbly, happy and, yes, even cheeky when the occasion calls for it. The knack is knowing when to be humorous. Try to be funny at the wrong moment and it can be disastrous. I have heard a medium tell someone in his audience, 'Your mother died of cancer, didn't she?' And then giggle nervously.

Ironically, Doris Stokes has communicated with me since she passed to Heaven. One afternoon at home with Christine, Derek and his wife, Hazel, had called in on a social visit and we were having a general chit-chat when suddenly I saw the spirit of Doris Stokes standing behind Derek. I had to smile ... here was a medium from the spirit world who had come to 'talk' to a medium from this earth world. Doris was in conciliatory mood and we patched up any differences we may have had.

Doris, I recall, passed on some personal information when Derek asked me certain questions to ask 'Doll', as he used to call her, to verify that I was truly linking with Doris. He also asked Doris what she thought of so many mediums who were claiming to be the next Doris Stokes. Doris laughed, saying she was unimpressed with these claims of 'the next Doris Stokes' and 'heir to Doris Stokes', joking that there would be more Doris Stokeses now than when she was alive. She finished by saying she was happily reunited with her husband John, and family.

Doris was totally comfortable communicating through me and quite chatty, too. I found her to have a good sense of humour and to be remarkably humble. I saw a side of her from Heaven that I was not privy to whilst she was alive.

The importance of verifying the true identity of spirit communicators is paramount. For example, if I have someone's spirit father with me and in his life he swore like a trooper, it isn't going to convince his son sitting in my audience if I tell him his dad is a very serious man. 'That's not my dad,' he'd be quick to tell me. So, if I can say, 'He isn't half going on a bit, swearing, laughing, joking. If only you could hear what your dad is saying to me ...' then that man's son knows I've got his dad! It also gets the audience going, they love it.

At first, some audiences may think I am being a bit rude or disrespectful at the expense of either the spirit person I have with me or the audience contact. At one meeting, I linked a young girl in the audience named Clare with her dead father. At first, I could see I wasn't convincing Clare that I really did have her spirit father with me, so I asked him to tell me something positive about his daughter. He responded by telling me that Clare had a white teddy bear on her bed which her mum had bought for her twenty-first birthday. However, instead of passing on the message in this routine sort of way, I said to Clare, 'Can I come to your bedroom with you? Is that OK, Clare?' She became very shy and was not quite sure what to say because she hadn't a clue what I was getting at. People started laughing as I carried on ribbing her.

'Come on, Clare, I only want to take you to your bedroom for a minute or two ...'

Then I explained to her how her dad was telling me about the teddy bear her mum gave her for her twenty-first. I know it might be considered a bit sexist to tease girls like Clare, but it made the message that much more interesting for everyone, including Clare.

It is especially satisfying for me when I can bring comfort to someone who has lost a loved one to spirit, as was the case for a lady named Sylvia Hillier. I am indebted to reporter Natalie

Gray for the following account:

A mother says she has had beyond-the-grave talks with her dead son who drowned in a river tragedy three years ago.

Sylvia Hillier says her son has even described to her how he died, thus offering a clue to the mystery of the death crash which baffled police and other experts.

Graham, her younger son, drowned with his friend, Anthony Cater, when their car plunged into the Thames at Shepperton. No one, until now, had been able to explain how the car ended up in the river.

Though rumours were rife, no one reported seeing or hearing anything on that fateful night.

Mrs Hillier, of Greenwood Close, Woodham, is now convinced she has solved the mystery, thanks to Keith Charles — a policeman and medium — who recently claimed to have also been in touch with tragic toddler Ben Hardwick.

Mr Charles, from Chessington, visited Mrs Hillier's home and gave her what she believes was a vivid account of how her younger son died.

'I didn't know him from Adam,' explained Mrs Hillier, 50, 'yet he came into my room and told me so much about the accident it was almost as if he had been there.'

Mr Charles described a security van going the wrong way up the one-way tow path with its headlights full on. He even managed to recall half the registration number.

'I believe Graham and Anthony swerved to avoid the oncoming van and, because the road is so narrow, they ended up in the river,' said Mrs Hillier. 'There must have been some sort of an impact with the van, because the car had a smashed wing when it was hauled out of the river.'

Mrs Hillier said she had quizzed her son, through Mr Charles, about whether he had been drinking that night. She was told that all he had had was a lager with a lemonade top. A post mortem confirmed that Graham had drunk only a small quantity of alcohol.

Mrs Hillier said her son told her he was OK, and predicted that his elder brother, Nigel, would go out with, and eventually marry, his best friend's girlfriend. Coincidence, or not, that is exactly what happened ...

(Following this tragic incident, Mrs Hillier successfully raised sufficient funds to provide a lifeboat for the Royal National Lifeboat Institution in memory of her son.)

I never did actually work with Doris Stokes, but I did work with Gordon Higginson. One such occasion was at the Birmingham Town Hall when I stepped in for the other guest clairvoyant, Doris

Collins, who couldn't make it. Another occasion was at the Glasgow Town Hall on 26 September 1984. Gordon, a medium for some 50 years, was President of the Spiritualist National Union right up to his death. That Glasgow meeting was the big one for me. There must have been nearly 2,000 people in the audience, but apart from the huge gathering on that occasion, I remember it for another reason.

Derek has a son named Ray who is a very good medium in his own right. He has a spirit 'helper' named Thomas. Derek wanted to know if I was going to have a good night at Glasgow, it being my first big night, so Ray was able to tell his dad that if he asked me for a name, I would reply 'Thomas'. Ray's guide, Thomas, would watch over me and make sure I came up trumps.

On the way to Glasgow on the train, Derek kept asking me to give him a name and thinking he was just amusing himself to pass the time, I said, 'I don't know. How about Mary?'

'No, no. Not Mary. Try again,' said Derek.

'Jack?'

No, he wasn't happy with Jack either.

'Tony?'

'No, no, no,' said Derek impatiently.

Anyway, he kept up this game for quite a while until he decided it was time for what we called a little Jack and Dandy, Derek's pet name for a brandy! So he walked down to the restaurant car and soon returned with two cups of coffee and two brandies.

'Give us another name, Keith,' he said again.

'Fred?'

No, he didn't like Fred.

Eventually, we reached Glasgow and booked into our hotel. After a quick wash, we went straight down to the town hall to check out how many tickets had been sold — over 1,000 and they were still selling.

'Great! Give us a name, Keith,' snapped Derek, still hoping I was going to come up with Thomas, but I didn't.

By now Derek was desperate and beginning to think my evening was going to go down the plug hole. In any case, I was getting browned off with his silly game, being asked to come up with a name off the top of my head every five minutes. So, we came to the point when the show was about to start, the huge audience was now seated and I took my place on the platform alongside Gordon Higginson. The meeting opened and the host welcomed us all to Glasgow. Gordon leaned across to me and whispered, 'You should be forming your link now, Keith.'

'Thanks, Gordon.' It was quite an occasion for me, a near-rookie medium on stage with one of Britain's best-ever clairvoyants and standing in for Doris Collins. With some 2,000 Doris Collins fans disappointed that their heroine was not able to be there, it certainly wasn't the time for me to blow it. Then came my introduction: 'Ladies and gentlemen — Keith Charles, one of our new and very talented younger mediums.'

I was on for the next 20 minutes, and much of this time I could see Derek Robinson looking at me from the side of the stage, still urging me to give him the right name. Then an extraordinary thing happened. As I stood up, everyone seemed to turn into gold statues. It was weird. Nothing like this had ever happened to me before, and I thought I was going to pass out. I looked again ... everyone in the audience and on stage seemed to have a gold aura around them. What could be happening? Was it my nervousness? Was it spirit or something else even? The gold aura images must have lasted only a few seconds, though it seemed an eternity to me. I called on spirit to give me some help; I needed a lead.

'Is there a lady here named Mrs Stewart?' I called out. As soon as the words had left my lips, I realised my apparent stupidity. We were in Scotland, for Heaven's sake, it would have been a miracle if there had not been at least one Mrs Stewart in the audience! The hall was probably packed with Mrs Stewarts.

'I don't care how many Stewarts are here, please raise your hands,' I asked the people.

I was drawn to one side of the huge hall, to one particular lady and, as it happened, the only

Mrs Stewart present. I told her I had her husband with me who was saying his name was — Thomas!

'Yes, that was his name,' said Mrs Stewart. From then on I just flowed with spirit contacts and messages and when I had finished I received a very warm reception from the audience.

Afterwards, Derek couldn't stop talking about the name 'Thomas' coming through with my very first contact and reminded me that he had been asking me all day for the right name. Now he could tell me why. We both thanked spirit.

When I am on stage I often do feel very close to God. I even feel holy. But when my psychic evenings are over, I just cannot stop talking and I can murder a drink. It's my way of unwinding from what is a highly charged state of being. Clairvoyance is very thirsty work!

Having said that, I am not much of a drinker but back at our hotel after that Glasgow meeting, where Derek and I shared a single room — though in separate beds, of course — we both fancied a nightcap. We asked the hotel porter, Ronnie, to bring us a couple of brandies. Then we fancied peanuts, so Ronnie had to go back downstairs to the bar, get the peanuts and bring them up to our room. By the time he had returned with the peanuts, we had finished our drinks and decided we could do justice to another, so off went Ronnie for two more brandies. We were paying him a generous tip each time so he didn't seem to mind the running around.

We lined up our bottles on a wooden shelf which ran round our room. Derek had the poor boy running up and down stairs virtually all night, so in the end we nicknamed him 'Run Ronnie Run'. Poor Ronnie woke us the next morning at 6.30am with a beer each 'on the house', thinking it would give us plenty of time to have our breakfast and catch our train which departed at 9.30am. Unfortunately, we dropped off to sleep again and didn't wake up until 11.00am. We missed our breakfast and our train back to London.

These particular stories have nothing to do with being a policeman or a psychic, but I tell them to show what life can be like for this particular touring clairvoyant. Because I know I have a spirit life to look forward to, I fully enjoy my earthly life, too. My experience is that too many clairvoyants take themselves too seriously, believing they must present a public image of total sobriety and dullness, as though for someone to believe in the afterlife, they must be seen to be boring. What nonsense! There is a time to be serious and a time to be respectful, as well as a time to have fun.

I have always respected spirit and they accept that I have another part to my life which does not necessarily involve mediumship. I have a good social life; I have even owned greyhounds on and off for 20 years, and I enjoy my friends and family.

Since retiring from the police, I have been given a regular slot on London's Liberty Radio, which is hosted by 'Diddy' David Hamilton. The show is structured so that I use my psychic, not spiritual, ability for members of the public who call in with questions. Questions such as, 'Can you tell me about my love life, job prospects, emotional problems?' As it is radio, and to make it interesting, it is necessary to give quick replies but, of course, I also need to be accurate.

Accuracy is essential, too, when I give my clairvoyance demonstrations at meetings around the country. At such a meeting in Hove, West Sussex, the spirit of a boy of 16, killed whilst riding pillion on a motorcycle, communicated through me to a young man in the audience who was quite obviously sceptical that I had contact with his former friend. I asked the spirit lad for positive proof to convince his living friend. The spirit boy gave me the precise time he had died — 11.35pm. It was spot on and to press home the evidence of the spirit boy's survival beyond this life, he 'showed' me his distinctive leather wallet, which I then described to his friend. The young man in the audience recognised it immediately as the one his friend had on him when he died.

On a question of accuracy, it was quite unexpected when I met Emily. Christine and I had invited Derek and Hazel to spend a weekend with us. During the day, the four of us had visited a craft fair. The day had been warm and sunny and quite relaxing. The strange thing about it was there had been many coincidences involving spiritual matters which we had not been looking for but which had just happened. Over dinner at home, we had spoken of these coincidences. As we settled down in my lounge with coffee, not only did I become aware, but each of us could sense, a strong, spiritual presence. It was not disconcerting but a little eerie as the temperature of the room definitely dropped a few degrees. This is not uncommon when spirit is present. We glanced at each other and I soon linked in to find out who was with us.

It wasn't a question of, 'Is anyone there?' but 'Who is there?'

The presence was not known to any of us as I was impressed by the spirit of a young woman who soon introduced herself to us as Emily. Christine grabbed a pencil and paper to take notes as she, Derek and Hazel began questioning Emily. She told us many personal details, not only about herself, but of her family. She said she had been a single woman who had become pregnant and that her child had been still-born at seven months into the pregnancy. As a result, Emily had suffered post-natal depression and had been placed in a mental hospital. We queried this with Emily and she told us she had died in 1912, aged 37, while still in hospital. Emily told us her surname was Jenner. When pressed she told us she was buried locally, and that she was with William. Derek asked her if we would be able to find her grave. When she replied 'Yes', Derek and I were keen to trot off there and then down to the cemetery to investigate Emily's story.

'You can't go to a cemetery at this time of night,' chorused the ladies. We had not realised how late it was. Luckily, Derek and Hazel were staying overnight so our search for Emily's grave could start the next day.

It was a bright Sunday morning as the three of us entered a West Sussex cemetery. During our quest we became separated as we read the various headstones trying to look as innocent as possible, and not like grave robbers!

I crossed a pathway, and Hazel was some 30 yards ahead of me. Derek was about the same distance away, behind to my right. I noticed that some graves to my left had fallen into disrepair. I was about to shout to Hazel, 'Have you done these?' but stifled my words realising where I was, and how disrespectful my call might sound to other people. I walked up the slight incline to these graves and in doing so I felt the strong presence of spirit. I looked down at the first grave and read the words on the headstone —'Emily Jenner. Died 1912'. I called out excitedly to Derek. As he joined me he, too, read the headstone and by now Hazel had caught up with us.

'Look, Hazel, what a knockout. It is Emily.'

'And just look at the grave next to hers. Emily said she was with William,' Hazel remarked.

We read the name on the headstone as one William Kent. We returned home to tell Christine our exciting news and later went back to take a photograph of the grave. Intrigued, Christine and I carried out our own further investigations. We went to the local parish church and checked their records. We sent off to County Hall and also spoke to the superintendent of records at the hospital where Emily had once been incarcerated. All the information that Emily had communicated was verified.

I was made to feel most uncomfortable when I was called in before my Detective Inspector, prior to my scheduled visit to Gloucester for a show. My DI had been contacted by a Chief Inspector from Gloucester police who had seen a local newspaper report advertising my visit. Gloucester was the home town of the notorious Fred West, the serial killer, and whether it was his naïveté or personal prejudice, he had contacted my Inspector to say I might consider cancelling my proposed visit or I could expect a rough ride from the locals who might ask difficult questions. I had no intention of cancelling.

Alan Law, a fellow medium, and Derek Robinson met up with me in London so we could travel to Gloucester together. We packed the car and set off; it was just one of those funny (as in strange) days. The journey went reasonably well. In fact, we had a little time in hand so we stopped at a Little Chef for a meal. We were laughing and joking and even the weather wasn't bad.

When we reached Gloucester, we needed to ask directions to the theatre. It seemed as soon as we started to ask about the theatre things began to go wrong. Alan, bless him, was driving and went the wrong way down a one-way street, then he took a wrong turning, by which time we were starting to meet the rush-hour traffic. We found ourselves in a particularly eerie side-road. We all felt it. Alan even remarked that the road had a bad feeling about it. Anyway, at the far end I spotted a policeman and suggested we ask him for directions. As Alan drove us slowly down this road, we were about to pull up to talk to the policeman when Derek shouted out, 'Blimey, that is Fred West's house!' We didn't hang around any longer than it took us to ask the copper the way, and to drive off.

Normally, when we arrive at a theatre, there is someone on hand to welcome us. We knocked on the front door, at the side door, resorted to shouting out, but still nobody came.

'We are here tonight?' I asked Del.

'Of course we are,' he replied.

'It would be funny if we had come all this way on the wrong night,' I quipped.

Derek quickly flicked open his briefcase and checked his contract. 'Yes, it's tonight,' he confirmed.

We carried on banging on the theatre door and after a couple more minutes it was finally opened. A large man stood there, very apologetic for keeping us waiting. 'Sorry, sorry, but the Ladies loo has broken and the water is flooding into the foyer. I have the plumber here now. Come in,' he said, trying to be cheerful.

It was a lovely theatre, but as we all trooped in we were hit by a terrible smell coming from the Ladies loo, and the overflowing pipes. Would it all be sorted out in time for the start of my show?

We were shown to our dressing rooms and there was a distinct feeling of a ghostly presence. We all commented on it. We were unpacking our bags when suddenly the dressing room door, which had been left ajar, slammed shut! There was an icy blast and Derek and I looked at each other a bit concerned because we both knew that someone from 'the other side' was definitely in the theatre with us!

But the show had to go on. Derek and I went on stage to sort out the microphones and lighting, but there was no engineer to assist. We waited and waited and it was getting close to the opening of the evening show. Then the engineer appeared, with a bit of a swagger that indicated he had been enjoying his refreshments a bit earlier than planned, but we did manage to install our equipment on time. As Alan got ready, Derek and I walked round this old theatre and confirmed our suspicions; there was no mistake, the place was haunted by the presence of a woman's spirit in the auditorium. Derek even thought he saw an impression of her at the back of the theatre.

When the evening was over, and it all went rather well, we packed and left Gloucester for the return trip to London. On the way home, I think we were near Chippenham when I needed to spend a penny. Alan stopped the car in a lay-by on a B-road and I walked to the rear of the car so that I could do what I had to do without causing too much of a distraction to passing motorists. But in my attempt to be discreet I stepped too far back and plummeted backwards into a deep ditch before my head came to rest against a barbed wire fence. I was muddy, covered in bracken and well cheesed off. But it made the day for my two travelling companions. I don't think they stopped laughing until we reached London and we all went our separate ways home!

•4•

Helping with Their Enquiries

I entered the CID office in Wimbledon Police Station hoping for a quiet Saturday morning. At weekends, 'rest days' reduced the level of staffing but because this was August Bank Holiday weekend, with officers being seconded to Notting Hill Carnival, it meant I was the most experienced detective on duty. I checked the crime books and put together my list of crime scenes and witnesses I needed to visit. There were 13. Lucky 13!

I checked my route and decided my first call would be to an off-licence where a number of stolen cheques had been passed. Arriving at the off-licence in Raynes Park at about 10.30am, I parked my car in the adjoining road and crossed to the shop to speak to the manager. I was in plain clothes so I produced my warrant card and introduced myself. As I questioned the manager about the stolen cheques, I became very aware of my spirit guide making his presence known. I picked up visual images of a man's legs, and shoes bearing splashes of paint. Although the name on the stolen cheques was that of a female, I could not get away from what was psychically a man's legs and shoes. I asked the manager if he knew the person responsible for passing the cheques, but he could only vaguely remember a blonde-haired woman.

'Could she have been with a man?' I asked.

'I am not sure,' he said.

'Was she with a man who may have been a builder or a painter, by any chance?' I was trying to fit the psychic image I was receiving to the passing of the stolen cheques.

The manager said, 'Now you mention it, there was a man with her and he did have paint on his hands. I remember that much because he helped her carry out the spirits she bought. He put the bottles into a cardboard box I gave them.'

The hairs on the back of my neck stood up and I quizzed the shop manager further for a description of the man and woman but he could only give me sketchy details of the woman. I arranged to see the manager again to get his written statement, then left for the other dozen calls I knew I still had to make. On my way back to my parked car, I was still conscious of my spirit helpers with me. I got into the vehicle and flicked through my list of appointments. This overwhelming spiritual presence was for a reason. I sat quietly and closed my eyes. As I opened them I was aware of some four or five houses with 'For Sale' boards outside in the road where my car was parked. I thought, as houses were for sale, perhaps builders were still working on them, and that maybe I should go and knock on a few doors in the hope of finding the fraudsters. I drew a blank from the first few houses I called on; I didn't even get a reply. The only house I hadn't yet visited was right at the end of the road. I was conscious of the 12 other calls I still had to make and a little reticent at not having found anyone at home so far. I was going to give this last house a miss and return to my car but then I was moved by my spirit guides to call on this one remaining house. I knocked at the front door, but there was no answer. I could hear voices so I went round to the back door. I could not see anyone, but I could still hear voices coming from a back room.

I was about to give the door knocker another rap when a voice from behind me said, 'Can I help you?'

I turned to see a short Asian gentleman and what I saw astounded me. His legs and shoes were exactly as I had psychically 'seen' them in the off-licence 30 minutes earlier, and there were splashes of paint on his shoes. For no apparent reason I said, 'Yes, David. I think you can.' (Why did I call him 'David'?) 'I am a police officer. I believe you know something about the cheques in the off-licence.' He looked at me somewhat bemused and simply said, 'Yes. What happens now?'

As I stood looking at him, I was awash with a psychic sensation that I had the right man. I arrested him and we returned to Wimbledon Police Station. When he was being booked in by the custody officer, I was even more surprised when he gave his name as David. At the police station, I recruited the help of two crime squad officers and I interviewed David. During this interview he admitted he had been part of a group which had been obtaining stolen cheque books, travelling throughout the south and exchanging them at various retail outlets.

With the help of colleagues over the next few days, we managed to arrest other members of the gang. We recovered some stolen property and members of the gang were each charged with conspiracy to defraud, and associated offences. Subsequently, they each received custodial sentences.

A police colleague, Robbie, put through a call to

me at Paddington Police Station. Robbie was involved in the investigation of a North London murder and the murder team had come up against a bit of a brick wall. Robbie asked if I was interested in trying to assist, so I arranged to be at the incident room the following Friday. As I travelled there on the Tube, I did so with some nervousness. This was one of the first times that a fellow police officer had actually contacted me for my psychic help and I felt under considerable pressure to come up with something worthwhile. Naturally, I wanted to create a good impression!

I met Robbie and after a few formal introductions I sat down and explained that all I required was a photograph of the victim in a plain, brown envelope. Nothing more. With the envelope in my hand, I sat quietly for a moment of meditation and soon started to receive psychic images and information. I was conscious of the vision of a young, white female aged in her late twenties, with brown, curly hair, being attacked by two men. The first of these men was the tallest. He was white, 6ft 2in or more in height. He had dark brown curly hair, which was untidy. He was Scottish and I could see him wearing a woollen jumper and trousers. I was conscious he had been drinking. His accomplice was older, aged about 40, a white man who was heavily built, with a podgy face and large nose. I could see he was wearing a white shirt. I was told he was Greek.

These two men had bundled this struggling woman into an upstairs or attic room where I could see she had been tied up and sexually assaulted. I felt good as I relayed this clear information to the murder squad detectives who sat looking at me in complete amazement.

When I'd finished describing this incident, which had occurred in a building I believed to be a hotel or similar premises, I looked at Robbie for a response. He said, 'That's a good story, Keith, but nothing at all like the one we are dealing with!' Robbie then told me the details of their murder case and it was obvious to me that my psychic information was nowhere near correct in any detail.

As you can imagine, as I made my way home I felt a right plonker! I was dejected and despondent. How could I have been so wrong? How could I get such clear information, yet be so wide of the mark? I was so confused and I spent most of that evening trying to evaluate what had occurred. I just couldn't understand it.

The next day, Saturday morning, I resumed work on the hotel burglary squad at Paddington. At about 10.00am I received an internal telephone call from the uniformed bobby at the front desk and the officer asked me if I would go down to the witness interview room to see a caller asking to speak to a CID officer. As the only CID officer, it had to be me.

I went downstairs into the interview room where the officer introduced me to a white female, in her late twenties. This woman looked remarkably like the one I had seen in my psychic vision the previous day and she was certainly the right age. She even had permed curly brown hair.

Imagine my utter surprise when she went on to allege that she had been the victim of a crime the previous day, perpetrated by two men at the guest house where she was staying, in Paddington, having forced her into an upstairs bedroom. They had tied her up and had indecently assaulted her. One of these men she described as being a tall Scotsman and the older man as a chubby Greek.

This case was not solved, and to this day I remain baffled as to how I received this forewarning when attempting to adapt my psychic ability to a murder. Was I receiving a premonition, a psychic warning, or did I just get my wires crossed? I will never know.

Detective Inspector Wilson, of the British Transport Police, Charing Cross, sounded a reasonable man over the telephone as he started to outline a case he was dealing with. It concerned the death of a young man, but DI Wilson was hesitant because he didn't know how much he should tell me. It was clear he wanted my help but he didn't know the 'procedure', or just how much information he should give me.

I stopped him, and explained that all I needed was a picture of the victim, sealed inside a brown envelope, and nothing more so that I would not be influenced by any other information. This procedure always follows a similar pattern when I work psychically. A photograph of the victim, or missing person, is placed inside an envelope, which is then sealed so that I do not see the picture of the victim. I then ask spirit to draw close to me and provide me with a clear picture of the victim and the events, or the incident. The information I am then given by spirit is noted by a third person. For example, a detective.

In this case, the envelope was sent to my home by DI Wilson. I sat down with Christine, held the closed envelope between the palms of my hands and she noted the information I received from my spirit helpers.

As I held the envelope, I was soon conscious of spirit drawing close to me. I was aware of a young, smartly dressed man dead in what appeared to me to be a well or basement. He seemed to me to have dark hair, aged in his twenties and I could see from the way he was dressed that he had been to a social function. I was aware that this young man had walked to a taxi rank, or to a taxi, at one point during the evening, and that he had also drawn cash from a bank cash machine before returning to the function. I was also shown by spirit that he had been chased by several men and that during the chase the young man had fallen into this well or basement. Spirit gave me the names of two men. Christine noted this information and many other facts. The following day, I telephoned DI Wilson to pass on this information. He appeared somewhat surprised at the detail I provided and over the next week or two we had several other discussions about the incident.

This case was featured as part of a documentary on a programme called *Sightings* put together by an American film company. It centred on the death of Sean Harper, a young man who had been found dead at the foot of a lift shaft. DI Wilson said, 'Our victim had left the party, had taken the girl to a taxi, had gone to the bank and got some money. None of these details was ever released and yet Keith knew them. He told us descriptions of people who worked in the building. He came up with around 30 points about the case, with information we never released.'

He added, 'There are lots of sceptics in the police force and when I told my colleagues about Keith's information about the case, it made the hair stand up on the back of their necks.'

Sometimes it is necessary for me to question my spirit communicators as much as I would a witness to a crime in my former profession as a detective.

One such occasion was at a show in Hampshire. I was in the middle of giving messages to a lady named Rebecca from a young man in Heaven, and as I was completing this particular message, I was struck by the power of a spirit woman making her presence felt.

She was a woman in her late thirties; she was 5ft 4in tall, with dark brown hair straight on to her shoulders and curled up at the ends. But as she stood next to me, her head bowed slightly forward, I noticed she was wearing an old-fashioned nightdress, full-length and up to her neck, with almost a ruff-style collar. I was conscious of her sadness, and as I looked at her I could see her throat was cut, which had obviously been the cause of her death. But who was she? And what did she want? I know from experience that no matter what the cause of death, not many spirits make their presence felt with such force and urgency.

I asked this lady her name, which she gave me as Jayne, and I asked her why she had come through so strongly. Jayne said she had been murdered several years ago and that there was a man in the audience who knew her and to whom she wished to be linked. As I conveyed this information to the audience, I felt this spirit woman guiding me to the rear of the auditorium to a gentleman who was sat in a group of four.

'Excuse me, sir, but this lady says you know

her and you recognise her description.'

'Yes, I do indeed,' answered the smartly dressed man, who I guessed was in his forties.

'Why do you want to speak to him?' I asked Jayne.

She said he used to live next door to her, that they had been neighbours. The man confirmed this. I again asked Jayne why she wanted to speak to her former neighbour. She said this man had been frightened by her death and the fear was still with him. The man who had killed her also lived in the same house with Jayne. The man in my audience nodded his head in agreement.

'That's right,' he said. Though her murderer was not Jayne's husband, but her lodger. Again, the man said, 'Yes.'

Jayne then gave me a name which was either Jez or Jess. I asked the man if this name was significant and he confirmed it was. He went on to tell me and the audience that Jayne had had a Frenchman lodger and that his name was very similar to Jess. He had been arrested for Jayne's murder. The man then thanked me for passing on this message. He said there was no way I could have known the information I had given him, unless it had come from Jayne herself, in spirit.

·5·

Famous and Infamous

ake, as an example, someone like Adolf Hitler. Can his spirit attempt to communicate? The answer is most definitely 'Yes', but if Hitler's spirit came through to me, my doorkeeper would probably keep him out. Perhaps it's one of the reasons that, as far as I am aware, nobody has ever made contact with Hitler's spirit. Having said that, you need to know that evil people do not become evil spirits and get sent to an evil place to become still more evil — like a factory of evil.

In Heaven, attempts will be made to put such spirits straight. Learning will take place but there is always the chance that a spirit with a great deal of evil still left in it will attempt to come back to our world through a medium. Personally, I do not believe that the spirit of Hitler would be allowed to communicate. He'd be kept away. Whatever the risks and, of course, there are some, I have never regretted that I chose to take this route of spiritual development. I have so much spiritual contentment around me in this world and even more to look forward to in the next, the spirit world.

Sport has always been one of my passions. In my schooldays I played rugby for Brighton and for my school, and I was quite hot stuff on the soccer field with a regular place in the Brighton Boys Club team. My hero was always Scottish soccer international John White, who wore the Number 8 shirt for Tottenham Hotspur. I followed his career in the newspapers and on radio and television. Then, on 21 July 1964, John White was playing golf at Crews Hill Golf Club, in Middlesex, when a storm stopped play. As John sheltered under an oak tree, it was hit by lightning and he died. Such a waste, he couldn't have been more than 28. Although I came to terms with not being able to see my hero any more, that figure eight emblazoned across his back, I always felt he hadn't quite left my life. It was as though in some way he was still with me, which I had to admit could have been the case because his memory was so etched on my young mind. Yet, I would be sitting watching the

Saturday afternoon football on television and I would have the strange feeling I was not alone in the room, even though I knew I was. Quite a few years later, I was to discover the extraordinary truth that it had not been my mind playing tricks.

Well-known medium Bill Marie came to my house for a chat and told me he was picking up very strong psychic vibes. Bill asked me if I was aware that a spirit named John White worked very closely with me. I told him how, as a kid, I had often felt that someone was in the same room with me when I was watching football alone on television, but I didn't understand this feeling.

'John White is the dead soccer player you idolised. He has been working closely with you for a long time,' Bill told me. For some reason, though, John White's spirit has never made itself known to me clairvoyantly. As a spirit helper, it doesn't really need to do so. Besides, it is good enough for me to know that his spirit is with me. Soccer star John White was my first spirit celebrity. I now believe that he has moved on along his spiritual pathway and has progressed. I am flattered that he should have chosen to help me for a few years.

After I became seriously involved in clairvoyance from about the age of 31, I became more and more involved with showbusiness people. One of the Sunday newspapers called me 'Psychic to the Stars' and the name caught on. I would meet stars at celebrity events, they would be fascinated that I was a psychic policeman and invite me for a drink or a meal to see what I could tell them. This is what happened when I first met American actress Leigh Taylor-Young.

She wanted to know more and asked me to dinner at her London hotel. Over the desert, I was able to link with her grandfather who wanted her to know that when she arrived back in America she should travel south to sign some important contract papers. She told me she had only found out about the contracts that same morning, and was impressed that I'd been able to tell her about them and the need for them to be signed as a matter of urgency. Before I left her, Leigh gave me a book entitled *One Way Out* and she wrote inside the cover: 'To Keith. Spirit arranges things beautifully.' She also gave me her American home address and asked me to keep in touch.

Sometimes, people need to know something from beyond the grave that is important to them. Take the case of champion boxer Freddie Mills. Over the years there has been a great deal of speculation whether he committed suicide, or was murdered. The mystery remains unsolved. Or does it?

The one person who probably needed to know the truth more than anyone else was Freddie's widow. She came to me and fellow medium Bob

Brunton for a private reading. Freddie's spirit came through to us that day and was able to convey to his wife, through me, what really happened.

Freddie talked about clubs, his boxing, he gave birthday dates and information which I could not possibly have otherwise known. Mrs Mills was very impressed and accepted that it must have been Freddie's spirit passing on this information through my mediumship. Details of that conversation with Mrs Freddie Mills must remain confidential because it was a private meeting. All I can say is that she went away a much happier woman, knowing what really happened to her husband.

Another boxer who came my way was Duke McKenzie. He was with a young woman who, I believe, was his sister-in-law and it was a relative of hers who came through to me in spirit. I was urged to go to the man sitting next to the girl because the spirit message was that if this man was a mechanic he would be the best there is. Spirit added, to be a good mechanic he must work hard and within two years he would reach the top. What a strange message, especially as that man happened to be Duke McKenzie — hardly a mechanic! Two years later, Duke McKenzie won the European championship and, during his fight, commentator Harry Carpenter said, 'Duke McKenzie is doing a real mechanic's job here tonight.' I was watching the fight on television and when I heard Harry use that word 'mechanic' I nearly fell off my seat. Duke went on to punch his way into British boxing history by being crowned world champion for the third time. Spirit knew he was a winner.

When you have experienced so many incidents like that, little snippets of true information or seeming coincidence, an overall picture is presented which leaves me in no doubt at all that they come from spirit, from beyond the grave.

Many of you will remember British comedian Bernie Clifton, a particular favourite of mine, but I never expected to come face-to-face with him in a little 600-seater Newquay theatre called The Cosy Nook which I had booked to do one of my shows. Before the evening performance, my manager told me to go backstage where someone was waiting who wanted to talk to me. It was Bernie Clifton, who I knew was starring in his own show at the theatre the following day. He asked if I'd mind him sitting in on my psychic evening, and in return he agreed to draw the raffle ticket prizes.

During the clairvoyance, a fireman named Johnson came through and, to begin with, nobody was able to identify him as a friend or member of their family. Then Bernie admitted he had known a fireman who had died, but he wasn't sure if his name had been Johnson. Bernie may not have been sure, but ex-fireman Johnson had no doubts. He seemed to know all about Bernie Clifton! Through me he told Bernie he had just opened a new bank account, though not in the name of Bernie Clifton. Bernie admitted this was true. Johnson then said that Bernie was just about to go off to Spain to work. That turned out to be true, too. After the show, Bernie told me he was amazed when I was able to reveal the information about his new bank account because absolutely nobody knew about it, other than the bank.

Of course, there are many who put everything down to coincidence, luck or sheer chicanery. They have no intention of believing anything, just in sniping at mediums. When I have been on tour I've had that kind of treatment, but I don't need those kind of people to impose their views on me. I know there is life after death; they have still to learn this.

The Born Again Christians, with their banners and their heckling, try to make mischief; and if it's not them, then it is more likely to be a lonely old drunk who has found his way into our audience with a half-full bottle of Scotch, wanting to make a point or two. That's all right, whoever they are who might want to knock us are entitled to make their point. We don't mind. The drunk will usually slink away, but the so-called Christians sometimes like to use violence, stabbing their banners at us or lashing out with their fists, to drive home their views. We're no strangers to that sort of treatment.

Right in the middle of message giving, a man stood up during one particular meeting and began shouting out that we'd all got it wrong. It was reported that he was a member of a well-known pop group, but I cannot vouch for that. What he didn't take into account was the fact that he made his protest to some 500 people already converted to the powers of clairvoyance. Nobody in the audience wanted to hear what he had to say, so they shouted at him to sit down or get out. He realised he was on to a lost cause and slipped away soon after.

Another little upset happened when we met a group of local people in Taunton, Somerset, who believed they were much closer to God than ourselves. Elder members of the Octagon Chapel, in East Reach, described our evening of clairvoyance as 'wickedness' and they did their best to stop it. Pamphlets were handed round outside the theatre protesting at our presence in their community, but the evening went ahead to a full house. In fact, Jessie Nason and I, both with an international track record, went down so well we were booked into the same theatre for the following year.

On 4 February 2000 I appeared on the Nicky Campbell radio show. I accepted the invitation for two reasons; first it was a live broadcast and was to cover a period of 30 minutes so I could expect a fair hearing, and, secondly, I had met Nicky previously and although his outward attitude was pretty sceptical, I perceived him to have a genuine interest in my subject. I did not know that, having been invited to the BBC, I was to be joined by Nicky's other guests who were the makers of Channel Four's programme *Trigger Happy TV*. Although I have never seen the programme, I am told it is allegedly a copy of an old idea based on *Candid Camera*.

Nonetheless, we were all on the programme together and whilst Nicky was asking serious questions, or at least attempting to, these two men were being particularly silly and immature. I do not mind a sensible argument, or sensible comments, but when the producer of *Trigger Happy TV* asked me, 'You are a psychic detective, so are you used instead of detector vans to find out who has got a TV licence?' it was pretty insulting. They were also insulting to Sir Ranulph Fiennes, the explorer, who joined in on a phone link. They asked him what kind of underpants he wore on his expeditions.

I can cope with the Born Again Christians of this world when I hear stories like the one told by television personality Katie Boyle about her husband, Greville. Katie has had proof that her husband is keeping an eye on her from the spirit world. He used parking meters to make the point.

Katie's husband died suddenly at 4.00am in February 1976. Then days later, and still in a state of shock, she was driving to addresses in London sorting out her husband's affairs. She recalled, 'What gradually became clear was that I was having no trouble finding parking meters. It was very odd!' In fact, it was something Greville had always stressed: 'Leave your car at home. You will never park.'

Katie continued, 'When another parking space appeared at my next port of call, I said out loud, "Darling, are you helping me today?" Then I challenged him. "If you've got anything to do with this, then I'd like the next parking meter to be on the right." It was there!'

Coincidence? Katie tried again. She gave Greville full directions but, as she approached her next appointment, the parking areas were packed. She said she gave a wry smile, thinking it wasn't going to work this time.

'Then I heard a toot — the driver of a parked car was pulling out and signalled me to drive in. I thanked him and backed into the space. As I looked up, I saw the number plate of the car in front. It was GPG — my husband's initials.'

Katie was correct. It was no coincidence. This was spirit at work. Our loved ones have the most ingenious ways of letting us know they aren't as far away from us as we might imagine.

There was no one better qualified to vouch for

this than the romantic novelist Barbara Cartland. Before her sad death, aged 98, on 25 May 2000, Dame Barbara gave me her own truly moving account of the way her husband Hugh found a way to prove to her he was in spirit.

'My beloved husband, Hugh, died suddenly on 29 December 1963, one day after we had celebrated 27 years of great happiness. He was a quiet person who hated publicity and, having loved me for eight years before we were married, he was the most contented man I had ever known.

'Once, I said to him, "If a fairy could wave a magic wand and give you anything you wanted, what would you wish to have?" Hugh thought for a moment, and replied, "I have everything I have ever wanted."

'He loved me deeply but he believed that death was the end of everything; there was no afterlife, no meeting in another world with those we loved. After his death, I had a message which told me he had been mistaken. I have written down exactly what happened so that it will help other people.

'On 31 July 1917, at the Third Battle of Ypres, Second Lieutenant Hugh McCorquodale received the Military Cross "for his gallantry and devotion to duty during the action. It was largely due to his fine personal example and skilful handling of his Company that the enemy counter-attack was delayed," said the citation.

'My husband was just 19 years old when he was posted to the 6th Battalion in Flanders. Two months later came the terrible slaughter at Passchendaele. In this battle, the expectation of a subaltern's life was 20 minutes. On 31 July there were 279 casualties in the battalion and Hugh was severely — almost mortally — wounded.

'In attacking the enemy trenches, he was hit with a sniper's dum-dum bullet which passed right through his right shoulder and out of his back, exploding as it went. This, among other injuries, collapsed his lung and smashed three ribs. He turned head over heels and lay out in no-man's land for 48 hours.

' "You were very near to death," I said to him when we married. "Did you see angels, hear voices, or even feel you were being helped or sustained?"

' "No," he replied, "I just felt very tired and far away from all the noise of the battle."

'During the second night, Hugh was carried in on a man's back and received a number of shrapnel wounds in the process. At the field dressing station, they treated only the shrapnel wounds, not realising he was injured elsewhere. He was carried down to the base, but the shelling was so bad that the stretcher-bearers dropped him continually, and when he eventually arrived at Number 9 Red Cross Hospital at Calais he was so covered in mud they did not realise he was an officer, and he was at first put in the Tommies' ward.

'When the doctors examined Hugh they said there was nothing they could do and there wasn't a chance of his survival. He was, therefore, as was the practice in those days, put outside in a tent in the grounds of the hospital by himself to die. On 25 August his uncle, General Lord Home of Stirkoke, who was commanding the First Army, was informed and he sent for Hugh's parents to come over from England to say "goodbye" to their son. Mr and Mrs Harold McCorquodale crossed the Channel and saw Hugh for what they thought was the last time.

'Hugh had fortunately been taken to a "rich" hospital which was run by the Canadians, and they gave him port and champagne when they dressed his wounds. The rest of the time he was under heroin. He lay for four weeks without food, in a state of semi-consciousness, and we now know that leaving him alone and letting him get over the shock was what saved his life.

'After attending five hospitals and having innumerable operations, Hugh survived. He was a "showpiece" for the doctors, as they considered it a tremendous achievement that they had kept him alive, and he remembered being constantly "shown off" to visiting specialists.

'When he was discharged the doctors told him,

"It is a miracle you are alive. Nothing more can be done by surgery, so never let anyone fiddle about with you. You must trust to nature and live with your disability."

'It was advice he was to stick to all his life and gave him what amounted to almost a fear of doctors. Hugh was listed as 40 per cent disabled and received a pension which, at the time of his death, was £185 16s a year! His convalescence was very slow and when I met him first in 1927, I was told by various members of his family, including his mother, that he wasn't expected to live long, and that if he ever got influenza he would die.

'We often talked about "the afterlife". He didn't believe in one. He was a very quiet, gentle man, who never forced his opinions on anyone, but if I asked him what he thought, he always told me the truth.

'On 29 December 1963, after two days of slight bronchitis, Hugh got out of bed and collapsed. The scar tissues from the terrible wounds he had received in 1917 had touched his heart. I had always known Hugh's life hung on a thread and I was deeply grateful for having had him with me for so long. He did not suffer and for him it was the peaceful, quick death he would have wanted. But that did not assuage the ghastly shock and the terrible sense of loss.

'I had never seen anyone dead before — all my family had died in France. As I stood beside him as he lay in a blue bed wearing blue pyjamas, I could not believe when he had loved me so much that he had left me alone.

'A week after the funeral, my maid, who had been with me for over 25 years, said, "Have you noticed the wonderful scent of carnations outside Mr McCorquodale's dressing room?"

'"No," I replied. "Are you sure? There haven't been any carnations in the house since the funeral and those in the wreaths had no fragrance, not in December."

'"I was so surprised at the strength of the perfume," my maid went on, "that I called the daily woman and drew her attention to it. She smelt it, too, but said it must be something someone had put in the bath."

'I didn't think any more about this conversation, but the next morning I got up at eight o'clock as usual to give my son Glen his breakfast before leaving for London. There is an *entresol* with only a skylight outside my bedroom, on to which opened the doors from my husband's dressing room, his bathroom and the room in which he died. As I crossed the *entresol*, I was suddenly aware of the marvellous, almost overpowering, scent of carnations. It was unlike any carnations I had ever smelt in England — it was the true exotic fragrance of Malmaisons which I hadn't known for years. I stood for a moment feeling astounded, then had to hurry downstairs in case Glen missed his train. When he had gone, I came upstairs and the scent was still there, but fainter. I thought I must have imagined it but the following morning it was there again. It was, I discovered, in patches, the strongest scent being next to my husband's dressing room. Some mornings it wasn't there at all, or I couldn't smell it until I returned upstairs after breakfast.

'The fragrance came and went for three weeks. I asked a friend of mine who had been a medium if she noticed anything, not saying what I was thinking. She identified the unmistakable scent of Malmaison carnations and found it all round my bedroom door. I then knew exactly why it was there.

'My husband and I had always bought red carnations when we went abroad. Every year we went to Paris for a second honeymoon. The first thing we would do on arrival was to drive to the Madeleine. Outside, there were always rows of colourful flower stalls. Hugh would buy me a huge bunch of red carnations before we went into church and said a prayer for our marriage. This was something we had done on our first honeymoon and we repeated it every year, except during the war. The carnations would be arranged in my bedroom. Every evening when we went out to dinner Hugh would wear one in his buttonhole.

'If anything was a symbol of our happiness and our closeness to each other, it was red carnations. Now I understand why the scent of them was near my door. It could only mean one thing — that Hugh was trying to tell me he had been wrong. He had found a way to convey to me the truth — there is an afterlife; there is survival after death.'

Dame Barbara Cartland's spirit is now with her beloved, Hugh, in Heaven, together and probably for eternity. Her experience though, in her earth life, was the kind of very convincing spirit communication which many people experience after the loss of a loved one. There is no doubt that the strong earth bond of love 'pulls' spirit back to reassure those they have left behind that there is another dimension of life to look forward to; that there will be a reunion of our souls. I have every reason to believe that the spirit of Dame Barbara may well return in a similarly unique way to reassure those loved ones she has left behind that she is happy in the world of spirit.

Sometimes spirit returns to us for other reasons, as it did with Genesis star Phil Collins. In his case, it was to give him a warning that could well have saved the lives of his three children, Joely, Simon and Lily.

Phil says his late father warned him that a pair of old electric blankets he planned to put on his kids' beds were potential killers.

'Night after night, the blankets we'd stored under our bed were mysteriously scattered around the bedroom floor. It was scary. I couldn't work it out. Eventually, a medium told me it was a warning from my father not to use the electric blankets because the wiring was faulty and they would catch fire,' Phil told an American radio phone-in.

Is it all just coincidence? Is there some simple earthly explanation for happenings like these, as some will have us believe? Like the late Dame Barbara Cartland, like Phil Collins, I know differently. I know we live on in a life after earthly death.

It is this knowledge that brings such comfort to me in the passing to Heaven on 16 November 1994 of my 20-year-old son Mathew. He died on his way to work on his 'pop-pop' moped. A car coming in the opposite direction, for some unknown reason, went out of control and collided with Mathew. His death was instantaneous.

The days that followed Mathew's death seemed like a blur to me. I cannot say that we all feel the same way when we lose someone close; our experiences will each be individual. I found myself in something of a weird state, although I was conscious of what I was doing and what was going on around me, it was as if I was drunk. Waves of emotion would sweep over me. I would find myself sobbing uncontrollably or swearing at God and Mathew. I cannot explain it, I do not know why I reacted this way. All I know is that Christine was a tremendous support and help to me. A police colleague, Mark Randall, was also very supportive, as were other individual police friends.

I know that I was in some turmoil as to whether I wanted to carry on as a medium. After all, I was very angry with God. I thought, Why should He do this to me? I am going out doing His work and He takes my son away. I realised that it would have been easier to give up, but I took the view that, perhaps, through my terrible experience, I could use this to show others exactly what I believed in. I hope that people who lose a child will quickly realise that life does go on, and that one day they will meet their child again, as I will again be reunited with my Mathew.

·6·

Celebrity Contact

<u>Statement by the Publisher</u>

*The television presenter Jill Dando was fatally shot on 26
April 1999 outside her London home, and a man was
subsequently charged with her murder on 28 May 2000.
Several weeks before the murder charge, psychic detective
Keith Charles produced sensational psychic information
concerning Miss Dando's death — information that was
to be published for the first time in this book. With
regret, for legal reasons, these details must now be
withheld from publication in this autobiography.*

Keith Charles

It is the decision of the Publisher, therefore, that this information shall be kept in a sealed envelope and placed in the safe at the Publisher's offices until such time as it may be legally made public.

Although Keith Charles cannot comment on the criminal aspects of the Dando case, he does make some startling revelations about her new 'life' in the spirit world, someone special she has met there, and her attitude towards her death.

Jill Dando

As I have tried to make clear in other areas of this book, I have never wanted to tout my gift as a psychic for fear of embarrassment and insensitivity. It is for these reasons that I deliberately kept away from this case, and that of the death of Princess Diana. I have now decided to become involved because I feel sufficiently detached from past commitments as a police officer to be able to make psychic comment.

But as you have just read, because a man has been charged with Miss Dando's murder I cannot now give details of dramatic information I recently received from the spirit world, although I can reveal that Jill's spirit has settled peacefully and happily in the afterlife. In fact, she has been reunited with someone she much admired on earth — Princess Diana.

Yes, it surprised me, too!

I sat down quietly alone, holding a picture of Jill Dando, and said a short prayer. I was quickly conscious of spirit drawing close to me and was soon being told some amazing things about this equally remarkable woman. For example, that Jill had transferred a large sum of money between her accounts shortly before her death, and that she had been planning a personal trip abroad, a last-minute arrangement. She had also consulted a Harley Street doctor in the last 12 months.

But what about that meeting with Princess Diana?

I must stress that I have not had personal contact with the spirit of Jill Dando, although I did have an unusual psychic meeting with the spirit of Princess Diana. Or rather 'Diana' as she prefers to be addressed, and I will tell you about that later. But first, Jill, who made herself known to me through my spirit guide, Tobias.

She expressed surprise that she suffered no pain in her death, and she wants her family to know this, as she also wants them to know that she is enjoying meeting so many interesting people in her new afterlife. One of them is Diana. It struck me as quite funny, in a way, that these two women should come together in Heaven, but perhaps not so surprising because on earth they had so much in common. They both passed over in tragic circumstances, they were both great communicators, media figureheads, they got on well with people, they each had lovers and were not locked into just one monogamous relationship. And last, but certainly not least, they even looked alike. Two very stylish women. Jill says she would have loved to have had children, and certainly Diana would have had more children, too, had her marriage not failed.

If it seems strange to you that people such as Jill and Diana should meet in spirit, then let me try to explain that Heaven is where everyone can meet absolutely anyone else. Some have been there a long time, others only a short time. That is why Jill is so eager to let the loved ones she has left behind know that they will all meet up again one day. I am certain Jill has already been back to her mother — in dreams. They have spoken because Jill's mother wanted to know what happened, though the response was not the one her mum wanted to hear. The fact is, Jill doesn't want to talk about her passing simply because she knew very little about the circumstances that caused it.

And here's a strange thing ... Jill tells me that she is not very concerned about her killer being caught, other than that it will help her family come to terms with the situation. Jill says she has no interest in revenge, no spiritual vendetta.

There is always the possibility that a spirit with strong earth ties will want to return to the physical form, especially if it feels it was deprived of the experience too soon. But I can confidently say that Jill Dando's spirit will not be reincarnated, it will not return to the earth plain because she was an already highly evolved spirit when she was here. Her 'learning' is completed. I believe Jill's parents will understand this more than anyone; they would have seen that she had a degree of understanding of life and a knowledge of life far beyond her age as she was growing up.

Do those who die in such tragic circumstances as Jill Dando become troubled spirits and become earthbound? As I have said, not so in Jill's case; she has comfortably moved to her spiritual home where she is actively getting on with her new life.

She was a strong, physical person in her earthly life, someone who enjoyed making friends, and she continues to do so in her new world. Due to her strong personality and character, she has been able to communicate her spiritual presence to those she left behind, as her mother and her fiancé, Alan Farthing, would be able to testify.

Princess Diana

The temperature soared to over 100°F as my wife and I left Tutankhamun's tomb in Egypt's Valley of the Kings. Hundreds of tourists made their way through the dry, sandy valley where the preparations for an opera were under way. People from all nationalities were in small parties like my own, being given guided tours of what was a very spiritual and surreal place. Christine handed sweets to two small, local, begging children as we reached a tiny kiosk to purchase some cold drinks, then we sat down on a crumbling wall alongside others in our party, supping our canned drinks. Our tour guide broke the terrible news to us.

'Your Princess Diana is dead. She has been killed in London.'

He stunned us all with the news, adding that he had very little information other than that which he had been given by another tour guide. As it turned out, he'd got the wrong city, London instead of Paris, but shock and utter disbelief hit us all as we tried to speak to other tourists to confirm this dreadful news. No one seemed to know exactly what had happened, other than confirmation that Diana was dead.

Lots of rumour and speculation as to the circumstances of Diana's death circulated in our party but, as I say, it was the sense of utter disbelief that shook us all. When we arrived back at our Luxor hotel in mid-afternoon, we were confronted with a foyer packed full of other hotel guests, and by the concierge offering his sympathy over the death of 'Your Princess Diana'. We sat in the foyer for a short while to hear more details from an English woman who had seen the television news telling how Diana and her boyfriend, Dodi, had been killed in a car crash in Paris.

For the remaining days of our holiday, everywhere we went, from humble shops to large hotels, the local people offered their sympathy for Diana. It was as if they believed all English people knew Princess Diana personally, and it was clear to us that she was held in very high esteem by the Egyptians. Sadly, not all Egyptians we met seemed to feel the same way about Dodi Fayed, which I found rather odd. When I returned to England and became more familiar with the controversy surrounding the accident, several people asked me if I could psychically obtain information that would reveal the truth behind this tragedy.

At first I spurned these suggestions because I

did not want to be seen as yet another psychic all too ready to jump on the ego bandwagon. Some psychics who had given the Princess private readings, had been foretelling her untimely death. Also, I felt respect needed to be shown to Diana and her family, respect she had earned. I certainly respected her. Who could fail to do otherwise, especially for all the marvellously spiritual and charitable work she so readily performed? She had natural charm and vitality and good looks. And who would not be moved by the tremendous bravery of her sons, and the dignity of Prince Charles, who were borne along on a tide of emotion and passion that engulfed her funeral? I admit that, like millions of others, I sat at home and watched that funeral and, yes, I cried.

Even following this, with the ongoing investigations, the theories, allegations and accusations, I still did not want to get involved. It was only on one private occasion at my home that I sat down quietly with some close, like-minded friends and I finally asked for spirit's help for information about the tragedy. My spirit guide linked in and suddenly I was in direct contact with a spirit that simply identified herself as 'Diana'. Then I could see her face, only her face, and I knew it was Princess Diana. It was humbling. She showed herself to me with that coy, doe-eyed look for which she became so famous. An expert communicator though she was when she was alive, she said she finds it quite difficult to communicate from the spirit world, although she made it clear she makes every effort to show herself to both sons William and Harry.

Diana says she also found it quite difficult when she first arrived in Heaven, difficult accepting that she was really dead and difficult because it was her father who met her there. To begin with she said she could not reconcile the fact that someone with whom she did not get on on earth would be her first 'receiver'. She had expected another, but did not say who, although I had the feeling an angel might have been in her mind. She believed in angels. In fact, her conception of Heaven, she said, was different to the reality of it! Diana gave me the impression she was pretty upset that her life had ended in that French underpass, because she believed she had so much more work to do, her children to love and raise into young men, and a passion for life to pursue.

I asked Princess Diana if she was with her friend, Dodi, in Heaven. She told me, 'We have met, but we are not together.' Then she went on to explain that although they remain spiritual friends, they are both on different spiritual levels and pathways. She said that Dodi was met in Heaven by a man whose name was something like 'Saeed', someone who had passed over from his own family. She expresses disappointment that Dodi's father seems to continue to want to apportion blame for the crash. Diana does not want to apportion blame anywhere, or accuse anyone. 'It was an accident,' she insists.

As I continued to quiz Diana about the circumstances of the crash, she said that one of the rescuers at the scene of the accident took the driver's wallet and opened it, apparently in an attempt to identify those inside the wrecked vehicle, initially not realising it was Princess Diana and Dodi. Nothing was taken from the wallet. In another flip-over wallet, Henri Paul had on him a picture showing two children, and in his trouser pockets there were two sets of keys.

Diana told me that as the crash became inevitable, bodyguard Trevor Rees-Jones instinctively turned to his right and backwards towards herself and Dodi sitting in the back seats. 'He tried to stop me being thrown forward,' she said. She added that seat belt marks on his body would verify this. I have no idea if the fact he did this came up in the crash investigation. Diana did tell me that a part of her dress, which was cut from her body in hospital, was kept by one of the hospital workers — presumably as a bizarre sort of souvenir.

Of the men in her life, she wants Prince Charles to know that she regrets that their marriage didn't work out as she had hoped it would. Neither is there now any spiritual 'jealousy' over his love for Camilla, even though she could have forgiven him his indiscretions had he wanted their marriage to work. As for Captain James Hewitt, she says he was a shoulder to cry on at a very low point in her life, she was fond of him and she regrets he chose to take advantage of that affection. She has high hopes for her sons, preferring that they will not be drawn into the traditional military way of life, nor that of playboy princes, but rather to positions of influence where they can benefit those about them, 'as ambassadors of good', she says.

I asked Diana if she had any sentiments for bodyguard Trevor Rees-Jones, who tried to save her life in the crash. She is sad that he has been pilloried in some quarters, that his life has been shattered, and that to all intents and purposes he is now a broken man both physically and mentally as a result of the pressures put on him. She wants him to know that had she survived, she would have used all her influence to protect him from these pressures.

Tobias then took over, as an intermediary between the Princess and me, telling me Princess Diana and Dodi were two people who had both been affected emotionally by previous relationships; that they had shared parallel experiences on earth, both having been let down badly by those they believed they could trust. To the outside world, Dodi was a bit of a playboy who enjoyed the lifestyle created by the family riches. To some he did not appear to be entirely genuine — but he most certainly was with his feelings for Diana. He was an intelligent man who worked hard to achieve a good education. He was a man who was searching for the perfect partner. After all, he had a father who was known worldwide and a part of Dodi required a beautiful and as well-known a woman, or who was of similar social standing to himself. Dodi enjoyed his father's love and in an ideal world would have liked to have been even closer to him, the one man he most respected. Dodi believed he had met a woman in Princess Diana who fulfilled all his dreams, whom he loved very much. However, Diana insisted that despite suggestions they were to become engaged, the ring Dodi had purchased for her was a gift and not an engagement ring. She also insisted she would not have married Dodi.

Princess Diana had experienced a great deal of emotional turmoil since her childhood. Part of this helped shape the feelings of sympathy she held and showed for anyone in distress. She was a woman who, despite all the controversy and her sense of disappointment with Charles, still loved him. Diana had such a strong maternal love and friendship for her sons that she would never have put her own happiness before theirs.

Diana summed up the crash scenario in this way. On the night of the road crash, she and Dodi were both tired and looking forward to a good night's rest. When they settled into the back of their chauffeur-driven limousine, with Henri Paul at the controls, she and Dodi were not unduly concerned by the media attention they were receiving. She said it was not particularly unusual for her not to wear a seatbelt, and in any case she did not expect to be travelling at the high speeds which they later clocked up. There was little or no conversation in the car. Driver Paul noticed the paparazzi following and decided that if he drove faster to outrun them, his pursuers would back off. This did not happen and one team — a motorcycle rider and pillion passenger cameraman — actually kept pace with the vehicle. As it approached the tunnel, the motorcycle team overtook the car, the cameraman letting off a rapid succession of flashes as they passed which distracted Henri Paul. These flashes caused him to lose concentration and to crash.

I can also now reveal that Princess Diana did not die instantly, but I am informed by spirit that this was her night to go home to Heaven. It was a tragic accident; nothing more.

There was talk of the involvement of a small, white car. It has been explained to me by spirit that this car did not exist but was, in fact, the light-coloured motorbike which, coupled with the succession of flashes, created the impression of an overtaking small, white vehicle. There was no bearded man driving a white car at the scene before or after the crash.

Princess Diana has adapted quickly and easily to her new spiritual life. She has met and made peace with her father, and she has been able to meet others whom she admired in her earthly life. She has found the whole concept of the afterlife fascinating. Princess Diana has made, I am told, her spiritual presence known to her sons and to her brother since her death, and that she has appeared to her son, William, in a dream. Diana has said she will always be overlooking William and Harry's development, and will be close to them for ever.

Diana impressed upon me the significance of a chain, a sentimental gift from her to her son William prior to her death. This personal keepsake William cherishes as the last gift from his mother. Harry has two special framed pictures taken with his mother, which he treasures. One is a portrait, the other is a holiday snapshot. He keeps them in his bedroom, possibly not on view.

I felt quite at ease and comfortable conversing with Diana, who told me that she was at peace in her new world and was quite pleased to have lost the celebrity status she had on earth. She explained that on earth she did not initially court the press and media attention bestowed on her, but for circumstances somewhat beyond her control she was obliged to accept it, and later manipulated it to her advantage which she now regrets.

Diana had courage, a quality she admired in herself — a courage to speak out for herself and for others. She had not set out in her early days to be a spokeswoman, but her life was being moulded for her by a superior force, with her spiritual development in mind. Diana, as she kept referring to herself, has acclimatised to her new spiritual home and she loves to associate with those people she admired on earth; she has been fortunate to meet some of the great leaders of the world and is happy to mingle with those from ordinary backgrounds, too. Diana giggled as she told me that she is a most inquisitive spirit with a slight sense of mischief, eager to satisfy her appetite for spiritual knowledge by visiting some of the most highly evolved spiritual masters. One of her favourites is Xenthos.

I was intrigued to hear that Diana conversed with spiritual teachers and masters, and I questioned how she did this. Diana explained to me that in Heaven there are spiritual meeting places called *sumtas* (confirming something I had been told by Tobias and other guides, although I didn't know they were called this). She described a *sumta* by likening it to a large garden where there is a serene peace. The atmosphere is permeated with a fragrance which is apparently similar to sweet lavender here on earth. Her freedom to mix has pleased her enormously. She emphasised that she pays frequent visits to observe the progress of her sons, is pleased with their continued development and their growing bond with Charles.

Michael Hutchence

In the bizarre world of rock music, death and mystery have never been far apart. Idols such as Elvis Presley, Bob Marley, Jimmy Hendrix, Keith Moon, and Janis Joplin have brought notoriety and attention to their weird and crazy lifestyles. Most of these deaths have been explained to the satisfaction of their families, friends and thousands of fans. But can anything more be learned that will shed light on the mysterious death of Michael Hutchence? I agreed to apply my psychic detective ability to the situation and I was in for a dramatic shock!

I particularly liked the singer Michael Hutchence, and I enjoyed listening to him and his band, INXS. A bright young man, he was hugely talented and had many similarities to Freddie Mercury; he was once touted as Freddie's replacement with super group Queen. Michael's passion for Paula Yates created an embittered, tangled triangle between them and Bob Geldof.

Michael, I am told by spirit, was a sincere family man who cared very much for his birth family. He had struck up a good relationship with Paula Yates and her children and had a great love for them all. Michael always hoped to have his own family and was overjoyed at the birth of his daughter, Tiger Lily, with Paula.

I am informed by spirit that, at first, in their relationship Paula was demanding, being highly protective of her children and somewhat wary of Michael. However, there was a great passion between them and soon a deep love grew. Michael understood and sympathised with Paula's difficult position, struggling through a custody battle with Sir Bob over their children and coping with the intense media attention their relationship attracted. Michael was very supportive of Paula and she took comfort from his strength. I am told she was prone to wild outbursts when the pressure got too much.

It was Michael's deepest desire to see his daughter develop and grow into the beautiful young woman she will one day become. Michael was an excellent father to his daughter and he loved to relax with her and play. He was childishly in awe of his daughter because she had given him a part of the 'new life' he had longed for so desperately. Paula knew that in Michael she had met a man she could trust and who made her feel secure.

It had not been easy for Michael either when he ditched his Danish model partner, Helena

Christiansen, in favour of Paula in 1995. Michael was becoming a giant in the world of rock music, hugely talented, vibrant and intelligent and attractive for different reasons to both male and female fans. However, I am told that all was not well in his music world. He became tetchy and less patient with close musical friends because he wanted to get back on tour to perform live which gave him the huge adrenalin rush he loved so much. I am told he was looking for musical independence and was seeking out a new pathway for himself and his career just prior to his death.

Michael Hutchence loved his family — so on that November morning in 1997 when his body was found hanging in a Sydney hotel room, what had happened? My spirit helpers tell me Michael was suffering great loneliness. He was a man who did not particularly enjoy spending long periods alone; he needed to be with people. Just prior to the tragedy, Michael had spent time telephoning a few friends and family and he had eaten a light snack. Was he drunk? Not at all. He had a small amount of alcohol in his blood, probably equivalent to a few glasses of wine. Was he drugged? Certainly not. I am told he had taken a minimal amount of recreational drugs; probably a joint of cannabis. Michael had showered and had been wearing a black T-shirt at one point. His hair looked as if it had not been dried at the time of the fatal accident.

Psychic Detective

Strangely, the expression 'Indian rope trick' keeps being impressed upon me. I am not 100 per cent sure what this expression means, but although the coroner recorded a verdict of suicide, I know that Michael did not set out that night to take his own life. Although he caused his own death, by accident, the coroner had little option but to return the suicide verdict because of the circumstances. However, that was not Michael's intention.

Michael was taking part in a sexual practice, so I am told by spirit, whereby the intense sexual pleasure is heightened by the apparent tightening or strangulation effect on the body. It was this that caused his death. He was unable to free himself from the strangulation and died.

In my police career, I came across similar situations on a couple of occasions. In the 1970s, I was a CID officer on duty at Wimbledon Police Station when I was asked to attend a 'suspicious death' at a house in Morden. On my arrival at the neat, terraced house, I was greeted by the uniformed Sergeant and two constables at the front door and just inside I saw a white woman in her forties hanging by the neck from the stairs. She wore only a nightdress. Everyone's first impression was that the poor woman had committed suicide. I looked around the house for a suicide note, or evidence that I could present to the coroner; by the hall door was a postcard which had been sent to the woman by a lady friend, and the words which ended the postcard remain with me to this day. The sentence read, 'I hope you are still "pulling your strings".' A bizarre coincidence, or was it? As in Michael's case, there was no suicide note.

I have been asked by my spirit guide, Tobias, to express Michael's love for all those he left behind. I am told Michael has shown himself to Paula and wants her to know that he is sorry for the problems he caused her and the difficulties she has subsequently been through, but he will always keep an eye on her and the children from his new world.

Michael was a spiritual man who had a sense of fairness, was challenged by change, and was a strong character who would quickly adapt to new surroundings in his earthly life. He has found his transition to his new spiritual home both fulfilling and rewarding.

As I say, my first contact with Michael Hutchence was through my spirit guide, but not so very long ago, during preparation of this book, he actually privileged me with a personal contact. I was sitting in my theatre dressing room, preparing to go on stage for one of my shows. I was doing what I usually do, which was saying a prayer and linking with my spirit 'helpers' for spirit contact so that I didn't go on stage 'cold'. I was suddenly aware of a communicator with me in the dressing room wanting to speak. Then I saw him — it was Michael Hutchence. I was taken totally by surprise.

I could clearly see this man with tears in his eyes, but by the look of him he was otherwise totally at ease, maybe because he was quite used to theatre dressing rooms, having had quite a few of his own in his time! I still had to pinch myself to be sure I wasn't imagining things. Michael said quietly, 'Yes, I am Michael Hutchence.' He said he needed Paula 'to know things' and as he spoke, his eyes filled with more tears which spilled over and ran down his cheeks as he talked. He confided that he needed his problems to be resolved sensitively. It was so sad. In fact, as he stood there before me looking so vulnerable, I just had never appreciated that this 'hard' man of rock could himself be so sensitive. He said he needs Paula, her children and his own little daughter to know that his death was an accident. He did not take his own life deliberately. He told me that in his last hours on earth he had been feeling quite lonely, even depressed. He'd been wearing black that same afternoon, reflecting his sad mood, and he took a shower to try and pull himself out of a growing depression. But it didn't work, so he entered into his bizarre sexual practice, a form of self-hanging, hoping it would kick-start him into a better mood, a better frame of mind. It was not his intention to take his life.

Michael says he was becoming increasingly depressed by the fact he was unable to see as much of his daughter as he wanted to because of the difficulties. Now he would only be able to see her from afar, though he would always be around her, as Paula knows he is with her. His comfort, he says, is that Paula believes in life after death. She knows he is there, with her. He says he has been able to tell Paula from Heaven that he continues to love her, and that this has given her the inner strength to go on.

Michael told me Paula keeps a picture of him in her home and either has a candle burning near to this picture, or she keeps fresh flowers there. He tells me that Paula is getting deeper into some kind of mystical religion, too, and is getting comfort from it. Then he surprises me.

'You will meet Paula sometime,' says Michael.

I have to ask him if he really means me, Keith Charles. He says again that I will meet her, though I know of no such plans at this time. Perhaps Paula is thinking of visiting a medium.

Consulting a medium may well be among her plans, but Paula's Michael seems quite confident she has no plans, as yet, to remarry. He says she is still feeling too much pain and he blames himself for this, especially as his 'hanging' accident actually created still more problems for her. Then he said an extraordinary thing to me — that he might well be sent back to earth to help him rise to a higher level of spirituality. And he would like to come back. But this will not happen in the earth lifetime of his Paula. Before that, he says he wants to spend some time with her in Heaven, in a spiritual marriage, before it is time for each of them to continue along their spiritual pathway. Then he warns, 'But no one should take their life — accidentally or otherwise — before their proper time.'

Paula — your Michael is at peace with himself and with the circumstances that took him from you. He says he knows that eventually you will be together again. And he hopes this knowledge will bring you peace, too.

Lord Lucan

Sometimes it was difficult being both a policeman and a medium, as I found out when I had a spirit-inspired vision about the death of Lord Lucan, the well-known gambler wanted for the murder of his nanny some 25 years ago. I believed nobody could be truly sure whether Lucan was dead or alive, although there had been numerous unsubstantiated sightings of him in a number of overseas countries. But now I know for sure he is dead — because he has told me!

But let me start at the beginning and explain how I became involved in one of the most baffling of mysterious disappearances on record. I had a vision about his fate one afternoon at my home, sitting at my dining room table, relaxing after coming off a busy night shift. I was feeling quite tired, but when I had this vision I was not asleep, nor even dozing. I was fully aware of my surroundings and what I could 'see'.

For no apparent reason that I can recall, I suddenly became aware of what I suppose most people would call their 'mind's eye' looking in on a country scene, with the name Lucan and a place called Uckfield sounding in my head. It wasn't being called out by a human voice, but was more a sort of echoing. I didn't seem to have any control over what I was seeing, but I knew this was no ordinary dream experience. If anything, suddenly finding myself looking in on this strange scene made me more alert. I took a pencil and piece of paper and began to draw.

Curious about this brilliantly clear vision, I decided to drive to Uckfield unofficially to check the scene of the murder, as I had seen it. My sketch showed a large house standing on a hilltop and a large expanse of lawn running down the hillside away from the big house. At the front of the grassy slope I 'saw' a body — it appeared to me that it could have been Lord Lucan's — sprawled, face down, alongside what I can only describe as a large concrete drain, a section of what I believe are called storm sewers. A man, his legs astride it, was standing at the top of the lawn near to the house, a smoking shotgun in his hands and he was looking down the grassy slope at the body. He was wearing plus-fours, a tweed jacket and trousers. He was smartly dressed, a bit like a gamekeeper. The Lucan incident was before my time as a trained detective. When the murder took place at Lucan's Belgravia home in London in November 1974, I had only been in the police force for five years.

The last positive sighting of Lucan was at a friend's house in Uckfield. This was where Lucan had driven himself after the murder of the nanny, so I drove to Grants Hill House, in Uckfield, formerly the home of Ian Maxwell-Scott, a gambling friend of Lucan and cousin to the Duke of Norfolk. It was known that Lucan had gone to the Maxwell-Scotts, presumably for comfort, advice and as a bolt-hole while he collected his thoughts and considered his position. According to a newspaper report at the time, 'He arrived alone at the house in Church Street, just off Uckfield High Street and stayed two hours. Mr Maxwell-Scott was not at home.'

The report went on to say, 'Mr Maxwell-Scott's 38-year-old wife, Susan, mother of six, told of Lord Lucan's visit. She said, "I was alone except for two of the children who were asleep upstairs. My husband was in London and I was rather surprised at Lord Lucan's arrival. It was about 11.30pm. He came in. We had a long talk. He sat down and wrote two letters to Mr Shand-Kydd, his brother-in-law. He stayed for about two hours, leaving at about 1.30am on Friday morning. He said that he did not wish for a meal." '

Mrs Maxwell-Scott said Lord Lucan drove off in a car, but she told police she was unable to describe the vehicle. Lucan was never officially seen again.

I have to admit that the vision and the sketches I made were a bit eerie. I discovered that Grants Hill House was no longer there. The Maxwell-Scotts had sold up and moved away and the old house had been demolished to make way for a complex of old people's homes. When I arrived at the site of the old house, I was puzzled because my sketch seemed to be wrong in one rather important detail. The housekeeper in the old people's home, who remembered the original house, explained precisely where it had stood. Sure enough one very tall tree, which would have been alongside the old house, was still standing, but where was the tree that my sketch showed would have stood at the other end? There wasn't one.

'There used to be, but it was blown down in the October 1987 hurricane,' explained the housekeeper, apparently puzzled by so much interest in a missing tree.

I then stood on the lawns which are still there and which once dropped away down the hill from the back of the old house. Where the grounds ended at the foot of the steep slope, and where I had indicated I had seen Lucan's body sprawled on the ground alongside what appeared to me to be a huge concrete drain, was a housing estate. Further checks at the local police station and with local residents established the fact that the housing estate was in the course of construction just about the time Lucan went missing, so it was quite probable that storm drains had been on the ground where I had seen them in my vision.

There is no way I can say who I had also 'seen' standing on the top of the hill with the smoking gun in his hands. I have no idea if the previous owner even employed a gamekeeper or allowed one into his grounds. So, is the body of Lord Lucan buried under the storm drains on this Uckfield housing estate? Was he shot by accident, or even deliberately, and his body disposed of there? Was it suicide?

One man who knew the owners of Grants Hill House well enough to be paying regular visits to the house at the time of Lucan's disappearance was a local trader who, in more recent years, had become a traffic warden. He told me that he had heard most theories about Lucan's mysterious disappearance — other than mine, which he said he considered the most bizarre and yet perhaps the most plausible. If Lucan had been murdered, or had committed suicide, what better resting place for the body than in the deep footings, later covered by storm sewers underneath a housing estate? There is no way anyone is going to dig up a housing estate to try and trace a body which might have been buried there so many years ago. It would be almost the perfect murder, or the perfect suicide!

As for the motive for killing Lord Lucan, I was

only able to hazard a guess. As I have said, he could have been mistaken for an intruder and been shot, then when it was discovered who he was and what he was believed to have done, his disposal in this way was probably the easiest and safest solution. At that time, if you had asked me to offer a still more bizarre answer, I'd have said that perhaps it was Lucan's own wish that he should die at the hands of his mystery killer. Did he ask to be shot? Did he even shoot himself and stagger down that grassy slope? Maybe the man in my vision holding the smoking gun was Lucan himself, a moment before he died by his own hand? The man was clearly in a distraught mental state, with little future ahead of him, just a lifetime on the run from the police. Of course, this was all speculation. I truly believed at the time that the truth would never ever be known.

I never put forward my psychic theories about the fate of Lucan to my former police bosses. If, ultimately, I could not prove what I believed to be true, how could I expect the police investigating Lucan's disappearance to take my theories and vision seriously? Obviously I could not.

By coincidence, when I was working at Hounslow Police Station, I met an old friend from Hendon Police College. It transpired that he was a Detective Sergeant who had been involved in the investigation of Lucan's disappearance. Over a cup of tea, I put forward my theory which he dismissed outright, but who could blame him? I remained convinced, however, that Lucan committed suicide and that his body was buried by a friend in the foundations of storm sewers underneath the estate which borders the former Grants Hill House.

I have been questioned by TV presenters and newspaper reporters who took the sceptical view that if I knew where Lucan was buried, why didn't I pinpoint his burial place to the police? I would say that I did so in numerous television and newspaper interviews. But who would fund the excavation of a part of a large housing estate to check out my spirit information?

So, why do I now say so decisively that Lord Lucan is most definitely dead? Because, as I said earlier, Lord Lucan has told me so! Lucan came to me from spirit and revealed a great deal more about the case which has baffled the experts for so long. Hopefully, I can now give them some peace of mind, although Lucan doubts it. He laughs at their attitude towards the investigations. And in his own inimitable way, he loves the intrigue which his disappearance created.

At first I wasn't sure who I was 'seeing' when this fine flamboyant figure of a spirit man presented himself to me, although the moustached face seemed familiar. He told me his name was 'Lucan'. And there was definitely an arrogance, a cockiness about him that, after so long, still nobody has a clue where he really is. He loves the fact there is so much confusion and uncertainty.

At first I wasn't sure I even wanted to talk to this arrogant man. Was he taking the mickey because he knew I was an ex-detective? I was in two minds whether or not to carry on this conversation.

Anyway, he began to tell me that he did kill his nanny, that it was not an accident, and that she had not been killed mistakenly for his wife. He returned home tired and irritable to be confronted by the nanny with whom he was 'playing around', though not having a full-blown affair. It seems there was an argument, which could have been that the nanny threatened to go public.

'There was a loss of temper,' he told me, and he hit out. The nanny dropped dead. The seriousness of the situation sobered up Lucan almost instantly, and he believed his only recourse was to make a run for it. As he drove to friends in Sussex, he realised his life would never be the same again — the disgrace, the shame, the murder trial that would ensue, ending in imprisonment. He saw no alternative but to take his own life. It was the only honourable way out, as he saw it. Lord Lucan said he killed himself with a single gunshot that night in Uckfield and was helped by someone else, though I am informed that the person who assisted has now also passed over.

Lord Lucan's big regret from the spirit world is that he brought such shame on to his family, especially his son. He does not want his son to inherit his title because he says it is tainted. It is shamed. Given the situation over again, Lucan said he would surrender to the police and take what was coming to him. It is a regret that lives with him for eternity.

Robert Maxwell

Robert Maxwell was a big man — big in the sense that he was a physically large man, as well as in the power that his money could buy him, but despite his obvious desire to be powerful and popular, he never really achieved either. He was a Jekyll and Hyde character, a man who clearly cared for his family, but who took few prisoners in order to achieve his high ambitions.

Maxwell started out in life with good intentions but when he began mixing with the rich and famous, the power that went hand-in-hand with wealth corrupted his own moral attitudes. Power and the influence of wealth became all-important to him. Sad to say that many business people start out with good intentions and then, for various reasons, go off the rails, change their goals and, in turn, their true personalities. Maxwell was one such person. I am informed by spirit that, since his passing into his new world and his spiritual reform, he is sorry for what he became.

I have received spirit information that Robert

Maxwell's death, although by drowning, was no accident. The bottom line is that he died by drowning after being forced overboard from his luxury yacht *Lady Ghislaine* off the Canary Islands in 1991. His body was found in the sea five days after he had disappeared from the yacht.

Why, and how, did he really die?

Here was a man who was familiar with his own surroundings, who was not drunk, and aboard his private yacht in a moderate sea. A theory has been put forward that he committed suicide because he could not face financial ruin or public humiliation. However, from my spiritual communication, I can say this was definitely not the case. Mr Maxwell did not commit suicide.

I have been psychically informed that Robert Maxwell's death was murder, carefully planned and manipulated by assassins trained in underwater skills and techniques. They had spent days observing his movements and noting his habits. The newspaper tycoon's death was planned so as not to be an embarrassment to his political masters.

I believe he was mixed up in some kind of activity involving arms dealing and subterfuge with Middle Eastern countries. Because of his own mismanagement of his companies he had made promises, though not necessarily financial promises; more likely, promises relating to positions of power. Quite arrogantly he believed that by financing his illegal dealings from his company funds and readily accessible cash, he would be out of harm's way, having gained his own position of power and strength.

He was rejected by those who would have given him this political power and before he had the opportunity, by means of a possible suicide letter to cause 'political embarrassment', his political masters took the initiative and murdered him.

How did it happen?

A group of five men, highly trained in underwater survival and underwater combat skills comparable to those of Britain's SAS, had been put together by a Middle East power to remove Robert Maxwell. These assassins climbed aboard the yacht, took him from his bed and into the water some time after midnight. I could see one of them holding his mouth, others each holding limbs, so that no physical marks would show on the body.

He'd had a meeting a few months before his death with his 'masters', so he knew he was not going to get what he'd been promised. He was up to his neck in his own skulduggery over the illegal theft of pension funds, and failed promises from abroad. But his big mistake was to threaten these people that he intended to tell the world what was going on. He believed in his own importance, and believed he would get away with bullying those in power as he had done in business.

As it turned out, this was to be his biggest mistake of all. It resulted in his untimely death — or his timely death, depending on from which side you looked at it.

Suzy Lamplugh

In the Eighties, once I had become aware of my psychic ability, I decided to test my psychic gift. After all, I was a police officer used to dealing in evidence that most of the time was black or white, so having become aware of this gift I wished to reaffirm my belief in its power. If I was to become a medium and declare my interest, not only to my colleagues but to the world, I was the one person who needed to be convinced that I did have this gift from God.

I set up my own crude psychic test. This was that I would have friends place a variety of news stories — murders, missing persons, football reports — into a plain envelope and I would hold this envelope and link in with spirit for them to give me information about the contents. It was in this way that I received psychic information relating to the mysterious disappearance of estate agent Suzy Lamplugh after she had kept an appointment with a 'Mr Kipper'. I held the envelope and was very conscious of spirit drawing close to me. I could 'see' a girl I knew to be Suzy dead in the basement of a large terraced house. In the dimly lit basement room, face down on the bare concrete floor, I could see her crumpled, lifeless body. There were a few steep stairs going down into the basement which led into the room where I could 'see' the young woman's body. The concrete had a fresh look about it, as though it had only been down for less than a year. The walls were constructed of exposed brick, as though the plaster had been removed. I would guess the size of the room as about 12ft x 10ft. My feeling was that work had been started on renovating the basement, but it had been left unfinished for some reason.

A short distance from the house, I could see a large, grassed area and the name Fortesque Avenue. The presence of a grassed area near to this road and the mental impression I had of a square were relevant. After she had been strangled, Suzy's body was removed by her killer and taken out of London; I was conscious of that sad journey passing near to Ascot, although I did not get the final destination.

I remember being so unnerved by the clarity of this vision that I hurried down to my car to check out the name of the road in my London A-Z.

I was surprised to discover only one

Fortesque Avenue in the whole of the Greater London area, where there are many thousands of streets. As a psychic, I take notice of what my spirit guides tell me, and as this was such an unusual-sounding name and the only one in London, even though it wasn't in the Fulham area, there was a strong significance to this road, particularly as there was a large square green area within a short distance of Fortesque Avenue.

Information disclosed by the police to the public during the Suzy Lamplugh investigation tended to point to her death, or disappearance, being connected to Fulham. Therefore, as a police officer faced with my Hackney connection being so strong and clear, I went and told the DI in charge of the case.

I told him what I had 'seen', although I must say he appeared less than impressed. I have now been asked if I can give further information.

It is my belief that the person responsible for Suzy's death has been in prison for another unrelated matter and that there is someone else besides the murderer who knows the real 'Mr Kipper'. I see him as now being around 50, with receding dark hair, having put on weight and suffering from health problems, probably to do with his chest.

I have the deepest sympathy for Suzy's mother because she, like me, has lost a child.

Though in her case it is more difficult because she did not have a daughter to bury.

Richey Edwards

On 1 February 1995, rock star Richey Edwards walked out of the Embassy Hotel in London and disappeared. His car was found two weeks later near the Severn Bridge, a well-known suicide spot, but no body was ever recovered. Was a reported sighting in the Canary Islands that of the missing Manic Street Preacher rock star? Certainly someone believed it was. A patron of the Underground Pub in Fuerteventura believed he recognised the rocker, but when he challenged the stranger, the young man ran from the bar and vanished.

Another sighting of Edwards in March 1997 was reported on the Indian Ocean island of Goa, but it came to nothing. Because no body has ever been found, Richey has never been officially pronounced dead. In fact, members of the remaining Manics band are so confident he is alive and kicking somewhere, that they have set aside his share of the band's profits in the hope that some day he will turn up and claim it.

Richey grew up in the care of his grandmother

until he was 13 because his parents were unable to look after him. From a somewhat troubled start in life he went on to study political history at the University of Wales where he was awarded three 'A's at A-level. He joined the band after they released *Suicide Alley*, and during his time with the Manics it is said he wrote half the lyrics.

So where is Richey now? Is he dead? As I say, his fellow Manics don't believe so, and neither do I.

Maybe spirit knows, so I turned to my helper, Tobias, for information. The result was fascinating because I am told Richey Edwards opted out of one life on this earth, and adopted a completely new one, collecting some interesting attachments along the way!

But let me start at the beginning. Richey may have booked into the Embassy Hotel when he first did a runner, but I don't believe he actually stayed there.

The night he left the hotel to drive west, Richey was not masterminding his own disappearance and this was far from his intention. He was feeling the need for friendship and was drawn to his old haunts for comfort. I am told that he had stopped on his journey to purchase a soft drink and when he returned to his vehicle his mood had darkened. Driving a distance at night gives one time to reflect, and Richey became self-analytical. At the time, he was a young man full of independence, a genuinely likeable lad who was comfortable with his own company, but who found difficulty switching off and relaxing. This wasn't something that was exacerbated by his increasing fame, but he had always had a sense that he had to be better than he was. This was not caused by family expectation or peer pressure but by an inner desire to achieve and to do well to impress his friends and family. He was an earthy sort, liable to change without a great deal of patience, but who believed the ability to understand others was most important. Surprisingly, he was not materialistic. It is wrong to say 'was' in the sense that Richey has not passed from this life, but still lives. It is correct to say 'was' when describing his former 'life'. Having abandoned his vehicle, the next steps are unclear.

This was the moment when he suddenly chose to escape from his life as a rock star, never to look back. A troubled soul at this time, he was on the downhill road to a complete nervous breakdown, though this didn't happen until a while later. Spirit tells me he had a mental switch-off and set out on the first part of a trek across Europe, initially going to Holland where he settled for a while, busking and restaurant waiting to make just enough money to keep him going. It was in Holland that he met three other young people, two women and a man, who were to influence what happened to him next. They were backpacking their way to India and Australia, or it might have been to Australia and then India. They persuaded Richey to join them. All four travelled on a shoestring, doing odd jobs wherever they went.

I see Richey living in some poverty to begin with, in back-streets, almost like a waif and stray. Then he suffered a complete breakdown and was taken in by members of some kind of religious sect who restored him to good health. For the first time in a good while, he was comfortable, well fed and well cared for. He had escaped death by a whisker.

Somehow, he found his way to India — maybe through this sect — and that is where I see him now; a new person living a totally new life, probably, because of a kind of amnesia, unaware of his past life in England as a rock star with the Manics. The name 'Bahktar' seems to be important, although I don't know if this is a name he has taken, or it could be the name of the place in northern India where he now lives, a town on the border with Pakistan. Richey has taken the name 'Dom', so he might be called Dom Bakhtar. I just know that in the language where he is now living, the name he has adopted means 'little bird'.

I see him with a wife, a slim woman, longish dark hair, about 28 years of age. There are two children with them, although being about six or seven these would be too old to be their own children. Perhaps they are related, or adopted in some way. Though Richey's new life is a frugal one, he is very happy. In fact, he has never been happier. It is as though he has rediscovered himself. Where he now lives is an idyllic place; there must be water nearby because I can see boats.

Somewhere in his wife's family there is a doctor, or someone is connected to the medical profession. I don't think Richey — or should I now call him Dom? — will be wanting to rekindle his old life. More to the point, I don't think he even really has any recall of the life he left behind in England in 1995.

I can tell his former band mates that Richey no longer has anything to do with music, nor does money interest him, other than that he has enough to feed and shelter himself and his wife. It is difficult for me to pick up what he actually does to support himself because all that I get from spirit is that he leads a very basic, unstressed way of life — one that has brought him complete happiness which this troubled soul never really had before.

Concerning the possible Australian connection, I keep hearing Tasmania, which is off the coast of Australia and may hold vital clues to his whereabouts. This seems to conflict with my initial feelings that he is presently in India. So could it be that he went to India first and has recently moved on to Tasmania? I believe his friends might stand a good chance of finding Richey if they have a mind to do so. I would suggest they should initially investigate Bahktar as a location in northern India, then find a village which looks out over a lake and boats. An Englishman with a name like Dom might not be too hard to find there. But one warning — don't expect a warm welcome!

Shergar

1've always had an interest in horse racing which came, in part, from my grandfather Bill Chapman who, in his early life, worked for a bookmaker's to earn extra cash. I remember him working 'on the hod' at Hove Ground Stadium in my early teens. (The hod was the satchel that hangs beneath the bookie's board and in which punter's money is placed.) It was my grandfather's job to count the money and check it.

For me, racehorses and greyhounds in full flight look extremely graceful. I had never been to the Epsom Derby, one of the richest-prized horse races in the world, and one of the sporting calendar's biggest events for toffs and working men alike. So it was a day I looked forward to when, with family and my three young sons Mathew, Daniel and Michael, we all set out from my nearby home in Chessington, Surrey, to picnic on Epsom Downs on Derby Day. I think it was about midday when we arrived on the hill in the middle of Epsom racecourse and set up our picnic. It was a colourful occasion, too, with open-topped buses, a funfair, hospitality tents with bands and helicopters arriving with jockeys and owners alike. All this at the same venue. Thousands of people converging on this site in Epsom for one main event — the Derby.

There was a lot of pre-race hype surrounding the Derby itself and in particular one horse owned by the Aga Khan, named Shergar. Shergar had been the pre-race favourite for several weeks and he was at short-priced odds to win the big race.

It was a warm and sunny day and my young sons were dressed in shorts and T-shirts. We were all very relaxed and enjoying ourselves. My sons played happily on the grass as the hill filled with more and more racegoers, then at about 3.45pm, the crowd jostled for position and cheered their respective horses as the race unfolded. Shergar, ridden by Walter Swinburn, turned this Derby into a bit of a procession, winning as he was expected to do, so convincingly.

When it was all over, Mathew wanted to go to the toilet and I walked off through the crowds with him sitting on my shoulders to find the nearest public convenience. I remember walking through parked cars and hundreds of people spilling out on to the grass, some of them unfortunately much the worse for wear through drink. I guess it took about half-an-hour to find the toilets and return to my car and the rest of the family. When I did so, I was asked where my son Daniel was. I thought it was a joke and that Daniel was hiding either in the car or under a blanket. I soon realised it was not a joke and that Daniel had apparently followed me when I went off with Mathew. Squeezing between parked cars and the huge crowds, he quickly became lost. Like any parent in this situation, panic quickly set in. My panic was also tinged with fear because I had seen how many people were around, made worse by the fact a good many of them were drunk.

As I rushed around searching our immediate area, I asked people if they had seen my small son. A woman told me she had seen a young boy who looked lost and had asked him what he was doing. When he answered 'looking for my dad' she told a passing mounted policeman who sat the boy on his horse and rode off. I knew the day's racing was soon to come to an end and that thousands of people would be trying to leave. I spotted a uniformed police officer and told him of my plight. He used his radio and was told that a young boy had been found and was in the temporary police station by the main grandstand. I ran all the way to that station with a pounding heart hoping and praying that the boy who had been found was my son, Daniel. My prayers were answered. Daniel told me he had followed me for a short way, and had then lost sight of me in the crowds before the policeman put him on his horse and had taken him to the police station.

Little did I know then of the fate that was to befall Shergar, the magnificent winner of that particular Derby. Having successfully travelled back to his stud home in Ireland for what should have been a great stud career, Shergar was to be the subject of kidnap and a blackmail plot by the IRA.

In the light of recent newspaper stories that his skeletal remains have been found (as it transpired, it was untrue), a number of friends have asked me if I 'get anything' on Shergar. I asked my spirit guides for information and this is what I was told.

In his secluded stable at his home farm, Shergar was beginning to settle back into his routine. It should be remembered that he was extremely valuable as a stud and any future progeny could expect to fetch many thousands of pounds in the inflated world of racing yearlings.

I believe that Shergar's kidnappers overlooked the fact that race horses are highly individual animals, that DNA profiling would show up for years to come in any future offspring the stallion might produce, making it almost impossible to pass Shergar's offspring off as unrelated progeny. That was why, once this blackmail attempt failed, the kidnappers were virtually left with only two choices — set the horse free, enabling him to be found, or kill him and dispose of his carcass.

It is my spirit information that only three men were responsible for taking Shergar from his stable. They had been given reliable inside information of the stable set-up and routine there. I am also guided that one of the kidnappers entered the stables in the weeks before the kidnap day, posing as a potential purchaser of another horse to see the layout of the farm. I 'see' this man as 6ft tall, thin-faced, dark, with short hair, thick eyebrows, aged between 40 and 50, wearing a check jacket and whose name begins with the initial 'D'. I could psychically see him walking through the internal stabling area. One of the other two men involved in the kidnap was the driver of a Land Rover and its white trailer. The man was 5ft 8in tall, and of stocky build. The third man was in his thirties, red-faced and medium build. One of these men I have been told has subsequently passed into the spirit world in tragic circumstances. The horse was taken, I believe, under some form of sedation, initially to a dairy farm about 15 miles away with a railway nearby. I could 'see' Shergar standing in a barn area, tethered behind a breeze-block wall and out of sight of any passing farm visitors.

This was a temporary hideout and Shergar was moved the next day to another part of southern Ireland. I kept getting the name of Kerry. Unfortunately, the kidnappers' dialogue with the authorities broke down and I am told a ransom of £5m was initially suggested. These demands were not met and with pressure mounting on them, the kidnappers faced a dilemma. They had on their hands a most valuable asset which it was becoming increasingly difficult for them to hide. I believe the police search for Shergar was closing in on their hideaway and, to complicate matters further, the thoroughbred horse became ill. Shergar needed special treatment.

Finally, the kidnappers, knowing they would not be in a position to breed from the horse, were left with only one alternative — to dispose of Shergar. I am told the reason Shergar's remains have still not been found is that his carcass was exported, possibly to Spain.

·7·

Cries of a Child

Case History

In March 1992, in Toronto, Canada, Robert Baltovich was sentenced to life imprisonment, with no eligibility for parole for 17 years, for the second-degree murder of his 22-year-old girlfriend, university art student Elizabeth Bain. Baltovich has always denied being the murderer, and in 1996 began an appeal against his life sentence.

It was alleged that Ms Bain had become increasingly disillusioned with her relationship with Baltovich and met him to break it off in June 1990. She was never seen again. Following three days of searches by friends, relatives and Baltovich himself, Ms Bain's abandoned car was discovered a short distance from her home in Scarborough, near Toronto. A large pool of blood had congealed on the floor behind the driver's seat. Baltovich was arrested for Ms Bain's murder five months later. The Crown alleged that after killing Ms Bain, Baltovich hid his girlfriend's body in undergrowth and parked her car a short distance away. But when the car was undiscovered, it was alleged that Baltovich took Ms Bain's remains to a secret burial place near Lake Skugog, northeast of Scarborough.

More than eight years on, Baltovich's lawyers continued their appeal against his conviction, claiming that Paul Bernado, named the 'Scarborough Rapist', could have been Elizabeth Bain's killer, alleging that this strong possibility was never put before the jury trying Baltovich even though Bernado attended the University of Toronto's Scarborough campus at the same time as Bain.

was at work in Sutton Police Station, in South London, when a call came through for me from a man who introduced himself as Mike King. He told me he was a private investigator, so I thought his call must be something to do with my routine police work, until he added that he was calling from Toronto in Canada. This was some time in the Spring of 1998. Mike went on to explain that he had read a feature about me and my psychic work in a British newspaper. He said he was intrigued.

'Do you think you could adapt your psychic skills to investigate any nature of crime?' he wanted to know.

'I've been doing just that for a good few years in the British police force,' I told him.

But I was at work, in the middle of a complex investigation and, at that moment, surrounded by my colleagues. It just wasn't the time to discuss my psychic work with an inquisitive private eye 3,000 miles away.

'I would be happy to talk to you when I get off duty. Give me a ring at home after eight this evening,' I suggested.

Mike sounded a nice guy, and enthusiastic, so I was interested in finding out what he had in mind. Apart from that, he did manage to tell me he was a former City of London police officer, as well as having served on the Toronto force, so I didn't see him as a time-waster.

It was not uncommon for well-meaning members of the public with personal tragedies to ring me at work to discuss their problems. At the same time, I was conscious of the fact that my police colleagues were getting a bit fed up that my psychic interests were intruding on my CID duties. They were taking my phone calls for me. Some callers were so rude to my colleagues that when told I was not available, they demanded I ring them back immediately to help sort out their problems! No wonder I had a serious heart-attack on 18 November 1997.

Later that same evening, back at my West Sussex home, Mike King called again. His gentle Canadian brogue came down the line like warm treacle. His approach was equally gentle and undemanding, so it was easy for me to listen patiently. Besides, he was paying for the call so I was more than pleased to give him all the time he wanted.

'Keith, it seems to me you may be able to help in a murder case in which the body has never been found,' he explained.

Before he uttered another word, I felt spirit close to me. To try and explain this, I could feel the hairs on the back of my neck stand to attention, I felt a chill come across me and goose bumps over my body. There was an intense heightening of all my senses. I then started to receive a visual picture of a site which I believed had something to do with this murder investigation. Without any further prompting from Mike, I told him, 'The person who was murdered was a young, dark-haired woman. The name Elizabeth is important ... a young dark-haired man, the woman's boyfriend, whose name I believe was Robert, with a Baltic-sounding surname, was responsible for killing her ...'

I heard Mike draw a deep breath at the other end of the telephone line. 'Christ, Keith,' he said shakily, 'the murder victim is Elizabeth Bain.'

I continued, 'I can see a house, with an outline

of trees, with a large field in front of it ... there is a drainage ditch on a lower level than the road where I can see a knife, like a hunting knife, in the bottom of the drain ...' The images were coming thick and fast as I tuned in to the scene I could see in my mind's eye. 'I can smell a pig farm nearby, and the owner of this pig farm is called "Jentzen" or perhaps "Johnson", something like that. A red-faced, well-built man who had spoken to the murderer on the day of the murder. I believe the murderer said to him, "I am looking for a lost dog" as some sort or ruse for being seen by the pig farmer.'

Mike was dead silent, absorbing every detail and getting it down on paper. There was more.

'I can see this farm is on a highway ... I can see the highway number — it's 712. There was a diner close by, which is very important. This man asking about the dog has been behind the diner. Within a short distance, on the same road, there's a motel which has pink curtains.'

Mike asked me if I could pause so that he could take notes of the information I was giving him.

'Yes, Keith ...' said Mike, eagerly awaiting further comments.

'The name of this place begins with an "S", an unusual name which I could not get exactly, but the closest word I know is Saskewach, the legendary "Big Foot". I can see a large area of water to the north of what I consider to be the murder scene.'

As I talked and told him what I could 'see' he made no comment, but he later showed me the notes he took as I talked.

'Keith, would you mind making a sketch of what you have just described to me, and fax this across to my Toronto office?' asked Mike. I told him I was no artist, but I'd do my best. I drew the sketch and faxed it the following morning.

A few weeks later, Mike rang me again at home and told me he had gone to an area known as Lake Skugog and had found Highway 7/12. He'd also located the diner, a pig farm and a motel which I had described. He had spoken to the pig farmer who recalled police searching the area at the time of the murder of the woman called Elizabeth Bain. The pig farmer said he couldn't remember speaking to a man about a lost dog, but he did find a lost dog around that time. This stood out in the pig farmer's memory as it was the only time in his life that he'd found a stray dog.

Mike told me he investigated further and spoke to the owner of the Sanman Motel, who said he couldn't actually remember Elizabeth Bain and her boyfriend Robert Baltovich staying there, but he did express surprise that Mike knew of the pink curtains because they were a special purchase made by him and his wife, at high cost, when they refurbished the motel at the time of the murder.

Mike was keen for me to fly out to pinpoint where I believed the body might still lie. Unfortunately, as I was still recovering from my heart-attack I had to tell him there was no way I could get out to Canada until I was better. This wasn't because I was not interested, but I just didn't feel I could risk my damaged heart. I told Mike that maybe in six months' time I'd be well enough.

I eventually flew out to Toronto in February 2000 with Christine to help Mike with the bizarre murder of Elizabeth Bain, and to assist in some other cases. I was especially keen to become very involved in this particular case because of the really 'hard' psychic evidence I'd been able to give Mike King over the telephone in a murder that had happened some eight years ago, and for which a man named Robert Baltovich was in prison serving a life sentence.

Christine, Mike, a Canadian television crew and I went to Skugog on Friday, 11 February 2000. It had not been a very happy start to the trip, the day before, for Christine and me. We had experienced several problems over our tickets for the flight, the traffic to the airport in London, the weather conditions in both the UK and Canada, and then our luggage went missing. What with all that, and feeling tired from the journey, it wasn't an auspicious start to our Canadian trip.

Fortunately, as we struggled out into the Arrivals hall, Mike King was there to welcome us, smiling happily as though it was a warm summer's day. He didn't even seem to notice the icy arctic blast of wind and snow that hit us full in the face as we made our way to his car. 'Welcome to Toronto,' I said to Christine. We both laughed.

At our hotel we unpacked and showered as Mike had insisted we go out to dinner where we would discuss the plans he had made for the coming few days. Both Christine and I were tired, suffering from the five hours time difference and jet-lag. We had a bite to eat before sinking into bed at around midnight local time, so we'd been up for nearly 24 hours. We were quickly off to sleep.

We had to be up quite early the next day, because Mike had set up an appointment for me in the hotel to meet Joy and David Roberts, the grown-up children of a multi-millionaire businessman who had been murdered. They had heard I was a psychic detective and hoped I might be able to shed some light on the death of their father whose murderer had not been caught. I was able to give them some information, but this meeting with Joy and David had to be cut short because of the need to meet up with the TV people not far from Skugog. Television reporter Jennifer Fraser had been fascinated by the involvement of a recently retired British police officer and psychic, and wanted to record the events and my involvement as the investigation into the murder unfolded. Her cameraman Ross and sound man Andy were already there when we arrived in hostile weather. Some 3ft of snow had fallen and it was around -5°C, with a wind chill factor of -20°C.

We drove to the area of Skugog where the murder took place. Mike and I sat in the front of his car, with Andy and Ross and their equipment squeezed in the back. Christine joined Jennifer in her four-wheel drive and followed. There was no conversation in our car, other than Mike saying, 'We're getting close.'

I said to him, 'Very soon there should be a grid across the road.'

As we followed a right-hand bend and the road began to straighten out again, we bumped over a railway crossing. I said to Mike, 'That was the grid. We are close.' We drove on along a highway, then I saw the numbers 7/12. I became aware of spirit very close to me.

We reached a small incline and when we got to the top of it, I asked Mike to stop the car because I could see about 800 yards ahead, on the left, identical buildings I had seen psychically a couple of years before when Mike had first called me. I got out of the car, followed closely by the television crew who began filming.

The Elizabeth Bain case had apparently been high-profile, hence the interest by national television in my involvement. But it didn't make it easier for me to have television cameras bobbing in and out of view all the time. Although, having said that, I was so absorbed in the fact I knew I was at the scene of the crime, in a place I had never been to before and which I had visualised so accurately so far away from my home in England, that it wouldn't have mattered to me if there had been a whole army of cameras present. I felt excited.

As I got out of the car, I was drawn by spirit to cross the road. Suddenly I was aware of a female voice from Heaven crying so sadly, saying, 'Daddy, help me. Daddy, help me.' I wanted to cry.

I got back into the car. 'This is the right place,' I said, emphasising that there should be a pig farm to my right, just ahead. The motel and the diner, too. And there they were. We drove to a roadside restaurant where all of us warmed up with hot soup and a huge sandwich. I felt on a high of expectation.

Returning to the scene of the crime, the view seemed to me to be so obviously different and I was puzzled as to why it didn't feel right to me. But, of course, it would be different. I became aware that Elizabeth was alive when she had passed along the same road to the Sanman Motel, but she was killed before she had been able to return to where I'd heard those sad cries for help. I was filmed entering the motel where I said 'Hello' to the owner, a pleasant elderly Dutchman named Mr Wim. He confirmed my story of the pink curtains. Then we all drove to Hagen's Diner which was closed for the season. I insisted that Mike stopped the car because I had a strong urge to walk behind the building, though I was prevented from doing so because I wasn't kitted out for wading through three feet of snow. I told Mike and the television girl that something important to the Elizabeth Bain case was located there behind the building. I insisted that as soon as the weather changed and the snow had gone, a systematic search should be made there.

Subsequently, Mike confirmed that he had contacted the Canadian Police Detective Sergeant in charge of the case, and told him I had 'seen' something of vital importance behind the motel. The officer said he understood my reason for wanting to go behind the diner because the woman's key fob had been found inside a trash can there — evidence which had been presented at Baltovich's trial.

From the diner we drove back to find the drainage ditch where I had psychically seen the murder weapon dumped. I had visualised the murder weapon as a hunting-type knife, nine inches long, serrated blade. My job was made

Keith Charles

difficult by the large amount of snow which now covered the ground. I had to rely on my spiritual guides directing me to the right place. I went to the field in front of some buildings I had seen psychically from England. As I looked down the road, I could see the drainage ditch I needed to find. I indicated to Mike and the television guys that, in my opinion, the murder weapon was hidden in one of the two drainage culverts alongside the road. Mike noted the spot precisely, a 150-yard stretch of the ditch, which he passed on to Detective Inspector Mercier, his police colleague on the case, for him to authorise a proper search when the weather improved in the Spring of 2000.

Having returned to the UK, I was contacted by Joy Malbon of CTV, at their UK office. She wanted to interview me in London in relation to the Elizabeth Bain case. We arranged for her to come to Liberty Radio where I was broadcasting one Friday afternoon on my regular spot with 'Diddy' David Hamilton. The crew was introduced all round, made to feel welcome, and before we were shown into an adjoining free studio, CTV filmed me during my psychic hour broadcasting live to London.

Joy asked me how I came to get my psychic messages. She came across as being friendly and pleasant at first, until she asked, 'Why do you do these hocus-pocus stages shows?'

I told her in no uncertain terms these were not 'hocus-pocus' and that what I did was very important to me and to those who received messages of spiritual comfort. This interview was broadcast on Canadian television the following Sunday evening. Mike King received a number of calls from viewers keen to help.

Following my trip to Canada and Mike's liaison with the local investigating officers, I was informed that a search would be conducted of the area I had pinpointed.

At the time of writing, Baltovich was still serving a life sentence for the murder of Elizabeth Bain, and his lawyers are pressing hard for an appeal against this conviction, arguing that much of the evidence against their client is circumstantial and unreliable.

Canadian private investigator Mike King worked closely with the Toronto police on the Elizabeth Bain case and believes her death cannot be blamed on convicted serial rapist Paul Bernado.

King said, 'Robert Baltovich has been convicted by a jury and has served time in prison, and was one of the reasons I called Keith Charles. Over the telephone I said he might like to take a look at a case that was in all the newspapers, a murder without a body. Keith began telling me things, things he couldn't possibly have known. "Girl with dark eyes," he said immediately. "I am getting the

name Elizabeth ... The man's name is Bad ...
Robert Bad ... I can see him in a car going up to
town on highway 712." That's, in fact, Highway
7/12, where two highways merge together north
of a place called Oshawa, in the country.

'Everything Keith told me turned out to be
true, right down to the colour of curtains in the
local motel. I rate his psychic abilities as the best
there is — anywhere. He was phenomenally
accurate and there can be no question of
coincidence. In each case on which we have
worked, he knew nothing of those cases before he
spoke to me about them, so I know the
information he gave me was 100 per cent
genuine.

'As far as Keith's information about the
Elizabeth Bain case is concerned, I don't think it
will influence the appeal. I don't think it will help
with any evidence, unless something physical is
recovered with her body and this can be directly
connected with the convicted man. In the Bain
case, Keith's information will give the girl's
parents peace of mind which they badly need. It
is really why we are involved, for no other reason.
The case is closed.

'Keith has been involved in another case
concerning the son and daughter of a wealthy
murder victim, but this isn't, as yet, public
knowledge. It is still under investigation so we can
only reveal that Keith has been able to assist both

the two adult children of this murdered man, and the police, and he has been able to give some valuable leads which are being pursued.

'I am not aware of any other psychics in Canada who have undertaken this kind of psychic police work. As for the police, they will always give any offer of help fair consideration. This goes for the American police as well.

'The Canadian police now know quite a lot about ex-British police officer Keith Wright and his psychic powers, with me acting as the link between the police and Keith. They have been very impressed.'

·8·

Death Truck Tragedy

Case History

Troy Armstrong, 23, was returning to his home in Dunnville, Canada, with his pal, Dale Sammon, on 20 June 1998, when it was believed he was killed by a hit-and-run driver. According to Sammon, they were waiting to make a left turn in the direction of Niagara Falls when an older model pick-up truck bumped the back of their car three times. He said Armstrong stopped, got out and walked toward the driver's side of the truck.

It is not exactly clear what happened next, but Armstrong, apparently provoked by something said to him, kicked out at the pick-up. He was then allegedly hit by the truck's side mirror and fell under the vehicle's wheels as the male driver, who was not seen again,

Keith Charles

*veered round Sammon's car and drove away. Armstrong
died shortly after.*

*The day he died, Troy Armstrong had planned to
treat Don, his father, to a plane ride as a Father's Day
gift. Don wants justice for his son, and since his death
he has been doing everything in his power — so far
without success — to achieve this aim, including putting
nationally famous private detective Bob Rankin on the
case to try to find the elusive driver of the pick-up truck.*

1t was a bit of a reunion for three ex-
detectives when two former Canadian police
officers and me, recently retired from the
Metropolitan Police, met up at the Golden
Griddle restaurant, Hamilton, an hour from
Toronto, on St Valentine's Day 2000. Mike King,
Christine and I arrived first. We had nearly
finished our main course when in walked the
third ex-detective, Bob Rankin, an ex-Sergeant
with the Canadian police who was representing
Collins Investigation Services, Ontario. Bob sat
next to me and asked if I minded him taping our
conversation. I agreed. He took a portrait of a
blond-haired young man from his clipboard, and
from that point on things became a lot more
serious.

The identity of the young man was unknown to me, but later I was to find out that I was holding the picture of 23-year-old Troy Armstrong. It had a near-instant effect on me as I passed my right hand gently over the image. You, the reader, have had the privilege of reading the case history of this incident. I must repeat that I knew absolutely nothing when that picture was passed to me, other than it showed the portrait photograph of a young man I was told had been killed. How it happened, where it had happened, and why it had happened ... I hadn't a clue. Holding the picture in my hand, I said a silent prayer and asked my spirit guide, Tobias, to help me.

As I began to repeat the information being passed to me, Rankin started a tape recorder and began to take notes. It quickly became apparent that my story of what happened in the early hours of 20 June was rather different to the official police record details on a number of counts. I was able to 'see' that there were three men in the victim's car, one of them whose name I kept getting began with 'D'. The third man, whom I believed had blond hair, had left the scene before the police arrived because he was in possession of a firearm. I told Mike and Bob that the incident should have been treated as a homicide — a murder — rather than as a hit-and-run; that there were people in Dunnville out to hurt Troy Armstrong. It was related to drugs and other crimes.

I said the truck involved in the killing of Troy Armstrong was still in the Dunnville area and that it had since been painted a shiny black. I scrawled the word 'Ford' in big block letters on a yellow pad on the table in front of me. I was able to give Rankin a lot of personal information about Troy's relationship with his father, such as the fact that Troy referred to his dad by a nickname, rather than as 'dad' or 'father'.

At this point I was conscious that the victim, whose name I heard as 'Roy', was talking to me. (The fact that the victim's name was Troy was only revealed to me after the reading.) He was saying that there was a wooden cross on his grave and not a headstone and that the cemetery was close to mobile homes or caravans. Roy told me that some sports equipment had been placed in his coffin and that he had been buried wearing a sporting shirt.

During my reading, I was aware of Bob taking notes, but also that he was taking time to glance my way from time to time, giving me the impression he was weighing me up.

Strangely, from the moment I began 'reading' the picture, I picked up 'pain', the pain of being crushed. I said I believed the victim had been struck across his chest by a baseball bat. Yet, I didn't actually 'see' Roy as run over, but I knew his death had been caused by a crushed chest.

The tape recording was later played back to Don Armstrong, Troy's father, but I was upset that on our journey home, Mike King told me Troy Armstrong's father had been waiting in a vehicle near the restaurant anxious to hear the outcome of what I might come up with at the reading. I would have liked to have met Don to express my sympathy to him, but in his wisdom Bob Rankin had already decided it would best if Don wasn't directly involved.

'A lot of things Keith said turned out to be true,' Rankin admitted later. For example, the cross on Troy's grave was unusual in that it was homemade, and mourners did put a number of things into Troy's grave, including a favourite sports sweater. Father and son did, indeed, have pet names for each other. Troy would call his father 'young guy' and Don would call his son 'old guy'.

Bob Rankin, the main investigator in the Troy Armstrong case, spent 30 years with Hamilton-Wentworth police before retiring in 1998. He said that as a result of our meeting and my psychic detection, he had been able to put my new information on file. The search for the mysterious pick-up truck driver goes on.

Just before publication of this book, Keith Charles had an excited telephone call from Mike King in Canada to tell him he had just heard that the pick-up truck had been found.

'It's amazing, you were absolutely right. The truck had been resprayed black, its wheels had been changed, and new sides fitted. The vehicle no longer looked like its original condition,' King said. It turned out that the truck was discovered in a town not many miles from the scene of crime. It appears that a nearby barn had been used by a gang of young criminals as their base.

•9•

Trainer Trail

Case History

Thomas Mixon went missing in May 1998. His body was never found, but that did not stop Buffalo homicide investigators from pressing for a murder case against Mixon's former room-mate, 21-year-old Bulgarian Vladimir L Sokolov. The only trouble was, Sokolov had disappeared, too!

'It's among the rarest of occurrences where you proceed without a body. The best evidence of the fact of a murder is a dead body,' Erie County District Attorney Frank J Clark told a local newspaper.

Thomas Mixon's mother, Nancy White, said she would be the first to admit that her son had been no angel, that he had sold drugs. The last time she saw him was on 3 May 1998. Two days later, he left a distressing message on her answer machine: 'Mom, I really need to talk to you. Page me.' When she did page him, she told the police she picked up a message that he had gone turkey hunting and if people needed him, they should contact his room-mate, Vladimir.

Nancy White then telephoned Sokolov. 'He told me, "You don't know what came down?" He said he'd tell me in a few weeks, adding that they were in a lot of trouble. Vladimir was so nervous he said he wanted to leave the country.'

Mrs White allegedly said she feared the pair were deeply involved in a drug deal that had gone wrong. She said her intuition told her that her son was dead.

H aving been invited to Canada to help in a number of criminal investigations, this was a day Christine and I had set aside for ourselves, and Niagara Falls was our destination. We set out for the Falls on a beautifully sunny day. The clear blue sky and the heat radiating in through the car windscreen made travelling in our car a joy, but on the outside of that windscreen, the wind-chill factor sent the thermometer plunging to -4°C. As we journeyed to Niagara with our friend, investigator

Mike King, he told us that later we were to visit friends of his in a town called Williamsville, across the border in the USA. Christine and I had hoped to visit Niagara on Valentine's Day, but the weather had been too bad, so we were especially looking forward to this visit and to spending some time at one of the world's most famous beauty spots.

Mike said he had arranged for me to visit the homicide department of Buffalo police where they were interested in my help on a missing person case. Not knowing the journey times, Chris and I believed we would still be able to have some quality time at the Falls. First we visited Niagara on the Lake, prior to our arrival at the Falls themselves, which were stunning. The view took our breath away as we looked across at the snow-covered river banks and into the beautiful, deep blue water.

As we drew up in the car park, Mike King told us we had only one hour because he had told Buffalo police we would be with them by 2.00pm that same afternoon — not something Christine and I wanted to hear. Nevertheless we did see Niagara Falls and lunched in the restaurant overlooking them before Mike ushered us back to the car for our onward journey to Buffalo.

We had to cross US immigration and had to spend nearly as long waiting for clearance as we had actually viewing the Falls. With our stamped passports in our hands, we set off for Buffalo, Christine and I still disappointed that we had spent so little time at Niagara. I wasn't in any mood to do psychic work.

As we drew up outside Buffalo Police Station, there seemed to be a great deal going on. Police cars were double-parked in the street, uniformed officers (not quite as smartly dressed as their British counterparts are) coming and going. Numerous callers swept in and out of what was clearly a very busy police station.

Inside the building, we reported to a civilian officer sitting behind a screen. It reminded me a little of the ticket office of a railway station. I introduced myself and told the receptionist I had an appointment with Captain Joe Riga, Chief of Homicide. We were given directions and took the lift. Stepping out on to the second floor I was reminded of a scene from *Kojak*, or *Cagney and Lacey*. There was a long corridor with offices each side and a mixture of uniformed officers, detectives, suspects and witnesses. Although I am, of course, very familiar with British police stations, this was new to me and I found it all quite fascinating. We were greeted by a uniformed Inspector who accompanied us to Captain Joe Riga's office. His secretary led the way and we were initially met by a well-built, dark-haired, moustached detective in his thirties, a very smart and friendly man who offered us a cup of coffee.

He said, 'Better still, I will show you where the machine is and you can help yourselves. If you want a refill there is plenty here.'

We took our coffee back to the office to await Captain Riga. Christine and I remarked how warm it was, compared to the bitter cold outside. Within a few minutes, the impressively dressed Captain Riga joined us. He was good looking, well manicured and wore good-quality jewellery. He sat down behind his large desk and, after introductions, the Captain said, 'I don't know how much you want me to tell you, but we have a missing person.'

'Please don't tell me anything, but I want to tell you that this missing person is dead. Would I be allowed to see his photograph?' I asked. Captain Riga obtained a photograph and handed it to me. I said a little prayer quietly to myself and asked for my spirit guide's help.

There was considerable pressure on me because I had walked into a police station knowing no more than that they were dealing with a missing person, and I didn't even know what Mike King had told his Buffalo police friends. Even so, I did immediately pick up the fact that the young man had been strangled and had had his throat cut. And yet, as a policeman, I knew this was just not logical because by cutting the throat and strangling the victim, either would have been sufficient to cause death. I also told

Captain Riga that the person responsible had been arrested and released. Whilst I was talking to the Captain he sat straight-faced and silent. Mike King sat behind me taking notes.

Here is how Mike King noted the information I relayed from spirit:

> Boy's death by strangulation and cutting ... bronchial problems in childhood. There was a gang falling-out. 'Bulls' could be the gang name, or perhaps 'Bullnose' ... The name Bobby Joe is meaningful. Hard drugs involved.
>
> I can see theft of drugs from a hospital. A long-haired youth, with a ponytail, is involved. One of two children. A watch is important to him; could be that the watch, a present, is an important clue. Something about a memorial service at St Joseph's.
>
> Eleven o'clock hospital, Friday 17 to 19. Latino. Shallow ditch near road. Phone call. Command post. Drug convictions. Name 'Bobby' is significant. Split family. Catholic link to all this. August 8 or maybe 18 is important. Did not live at home when he went missing — in temporary accommodation. He had unique nasal speech ...

As I continued, my sensitivity to the scene and those involved increased still further.

The suspect has two vehicles. Mixon's body was transported in a pickup. Is one suspect 27 years old? Another 25? Dead man had $300 on him. I could see a Velcro wallet with a girl's picture and identification in it. Burnt on fire?

There's a piece of orange material around fire from jacket or shirt. Ripped out label. Conversation on a gravel driveway — then boy was killed. Bad business deal. Machine such as a lawnmower involved somehow. I get the word Dubrovnik. What is the word for 'bull' in Bulgarian?

At this point, Captain Riga picked up the phone to call a Bulgarian interpreter and asked for the Bulgarian word for 'bull'.

I see a rip-off, or some kind of cheating involved. Suspect is hot-tempered. I see a shoe fragment at 3.58pm.

Murder weapon is in a drain hole near fire scene. Suspect brought in was questioned by an officer who does not live in Buffalo. An arm injury, left arm. Tattoos of 'dragon'. Police walked over grave. Sneaker size 11–12 involved.

I see ships (Navy) from park and go down — can drive from there to it. There are deer running free in this park. Mixon was killed there, never called Thomas. Liked guns. Had a fascination with them.

Cabin? Above rocks for refreshment sale. Beers? Drain set in concrete on site. Is there a North Road in area? Dead man had some kind of connection with naval ships. He was an arrogant boy and aggressive.

Suspect arrested within three to four weeks after inquiry started — discipline problems. Suspect in mid-twenties, dark hair.

Having read these notes, you can see that the information I am given by spirit does not follow any chronological order, or sometimes even a sensible pattern. It is my job to collate and disseminate it in a comprehensible way.

The 'coffee detective', as I later came to call him in conversations with Chris, stood in the corner looking on. I was particularly aware that the murder victim had, at one time, been in a vehicle with his murderer and that they had been in a park. Close by was a police post. But then I was struck by the victim speaking to me, saying, 'The police had walked over his grave and were in possession of his trainer.'

This use of the word 'trainer' caused a slight problem at first. Americans and Canadians call them 'sneakers', but good old Mike King was able to interpret for me! I gave the English size of the trainer as 11. Captain Riga told me the police were not in possession of a trainer associated with the crime but I still insisted they had it. Riga was equally adamant that I was wrong. Not in any hostile way, mind you, but quite firmly. He did say that Detective James Giardina, the officer working on the case, would join us shortly, just as soon as he returned to the station.

Captain Riga asked me to pause because I was coming up with information of which he had no knowledge. He went to find out when Detective Giardina would be back and, in fact, they both returned about ten minutes later. The latter was a shorter man, in smart, casual dress and he sat down in a chair next to Christine, folding his left leg over his right as he did so. This movement exposed his small firearm holstered to his left ankle. Christine looked on in fascination and when Giardina noticed Chris was looking, he said, 'Sorry, ma'am. Does this offend you? I apologise.' As he hurriedly placed his foot back on the floor, Christine said, 'No, don't be silly. I am just fascinated. I've only ever seen armed detectives on television.'

Captain Riga introduced us, then said to Giardina, 'Keith insists we have a sneaker belonging to the victim. I have told him we do not.'

I told Giardina, 'The victim tells me he was known by a nickname and that you have been to search a warehouse.' The detective sat expressionless. I added, 'The victim tells me there

was a fire behind the warehouse, a large one
where I can see railway sleepers being burned.
And he tells me you took the trainer from there.'

Giardina said nothing. I offered to sketch the
location of the warehouse, and I marked the fire
scene on the sketch, along with a brief layout of
the warehouse and other items. I handed the
sketch to Giardina, 'How's that then? You have
been there.'

The detective smiled and commented, 'Pretty
good.' He asked to be excused, saying he needed
to go to his desk. When he returned, he was
holding the toe end of a trainer. I said, 'That's
the trainer you took from the fire, isn't it?'

He looked at me and said, 'Yes.'

'That sneaker came from the fire?' Riga asked
Giardina, who nodded.

Riga turned to me and added: 'I am sorry,
Keith, I really didn't know we had it. That's
incredible!'

This reading lasted about one hour during
which time Mike King took four pages of notes
which he copied and handed to Captain Riga.

Having been totally absorbed by this reading
for Buffalo police, I could not get the case out of
my mind the next day. I told Chris and asked her
if she would mind taking a walk round the shops
at Woodbine Mall with me as I wanted to make
my own investigation into the trainer and the
knife used in the slaying of Mixon. At the mall,

we sought out several sports shops in an effort to identify the trainer. I had the image of the pattern on the sole of the trainer indelibly printed on my mind.

I was not having much luck, but in a shop on the ground floor of the mall I spoke to a shop assistant. He was a very polite, black male, trendily dressed, and in his mid-twenties. He immediately recognised the pattern and style of the trainers I had described as being manufactured by Nike which had not been stocked for about two years, but he had, in fact, owned a similar pair. I noted the name and style of the trainer before thanking him and leaving. Having identified the trainer to my satisfaction, I now wanted to do the same with the knife. I was surprised to find quite a large retail outfit which stocked hundreds of knives of all varieties, from small penknives to large hunting knives — horrible things! I chose a quiet time to speak to the owner of the shop. I had to be somewhat deceitful in discussing with the owner why I was asking so many questions and passed it off by saying that my son had once owned one but had lost it. I wished to replace it by way of a surprise. I could see clearly in my mind's eye a small, black-handled knife with a short blade of about three inches that curved in an unusual way at the end of the blade. The owner was very helpful, taking from various cabinets and displays a number of knives until eventually I saw the one I wanted. I noted the maker's name and style, once again, before I left. I felt quite guilty that I hadn't made a purchase because of the time the owner had spent trying to please me.

Happy to have discovered the details I wanted, when we returned to the hotel I immediately telephoned Mike King to inform him of my discoveries and asked him to pass these on to Captain Riga.

I am aware that the person responsible has fled the USA, but I am sure he will be brought to justice in due course, following the discovery of Mixon's body and further physical evidence.

As this book was going to press, I was due to return to Buffalo in August 2000 to do further work on the Mixon case for a television documentary.

•10•

Death of the 'Little Doll'

Case History

When the body of blonde JonBenet Ramsey, pageant baby and former 'Little Miss Colorado' was found strangled and battered in the basement of her Boulder, Colorado, family home on Boxing Day 1996, the brutal nature of the case touched the hearts and souls of all America, and later many other countries around the world. JonBenet was a beautiful little girl of six, a child who had so much to live for but who died with a garrotte around her neck and who suffered a four-inch-long skull fracture, the result of a brutal clubbing.

Nearly four years on, this little girl's murder is still unsolved. Even her own parents, John and Patsy Ramsey, have been placed under the microscope, and yet even after detailed examination of a bizarre note left by the killer, numerous theories and many scientific tests, the culprit has escaped detection. Despite nearly four years of speculation, one of America's most savage murders remains a mystery.

During the run-up to Christmas 1996, there was great excitement in the Ramsey family because it was party time. The Ramseys had hosted two earlier adult parties in December and now, on 23 December, it was the children's turn. JonBenet and her brother, Burke (aged nine), were being joined by 11 of their friends, and 23 adults. That's 34 people in all, including 'Santa' and his wife. A full house. By 8.00pm that evening, it was all over and everyone went home, having had a good time.

Christmas Eve was much the same in the Ramsey household as it is in most family homes. Preparation for Christmas Day. It was reported that for much of the twenty-fourth JonBenet was not with her parents, but at the home of a little girlfriend. That gave her mother, Patsy, time to drop off gifts, see visitors and prepare for her family to leave Boulder the morning after Christmas to spend time in Charlevoix. In her Christmas letter to friends, she wrote about her daughter, 'JonBenet is enjoying her first year in "real school". Kindergarten in the Core Knowledge program is fast paced and five full days a week. She has already been moved ahead to first grade maths. She continues to enjoy participating in talent and modeling pageants. She was named "America's Royale Tony Miss" last summer and is

Colorado's Little Miss Christmas. Her teacher says she is so outgoing that she will never have trouble delivering an oral book report!'

Tragically, those friends would receive this letter bearing the family news the day after Christmas, only hours before the calls went out to tell them of JonBenet's murder.

According to John Ramsey, his two children, Burke and JonBenet, started Christmas Day getting their parents out of bed to open the presents. JonBenet received a bicycle, and reportedly an ID bracelet bearing her name and the date 12/25/1996. She also received a small gold cross, a gold ring and jewellery. Around 9.00am that morning, Patsy spoke over the telephone to Shirley Brady, a former nanny and family friend, at her home in Atlanta. Mrs Brady said she could hear the children in the background and that Patsy had told her that the four of them were having a quiet Christmas morning, and that her husband, John, was clearing snow off the patio so that JonBenet could try out her new bicycle.

Pam Paugh, Patsy's sister, said she spoke to JonBenet on the telephone. The little girl thanked her for her gift, the gold cross and a chain — the same cross she was wearing when she was murdered only a few hours later. She told her aunt she had been riding her bike inside the house because there was too much snow on the pathways, though she was seen riding it outside later.

On Christmas Day evening, the Ramseys had dinner with family friends. The children played upstairs. They all left there at about 9.30pm, but didn't go straight home. They dropped off gifts to two other families. Before they finally reached home at around 10.00pm, JonBenet had fallen asleep on the back seat of the car so John had to carry his sleeping daughter to her room. Patsy then prepared her for bed. She has said, 'I undressed her down to her little knit top that she had on and put some long underwear bottoms on her and tucked her in real tight and kissed her goodnight.'

Then she said the short prayer that JonBenet usually said with her:

Now I lay me down to sleep.
I pray the Lord my soul to keep.
If I should die before I wake,
I pray the Lord my soul to take.

It was the last time Patsy or John say they saw their daughter alive. They went to bed soon after, telling the police they believed the house was securely locked. The following morning, they discovered their daughter was not in her room. Her strangled body was later found by John Ramsey in the basement of their luxury home some eight hours after a sinister handwritten ransom note was found on the stairs by Patsy Ramsey.

This note read (including spelling mistakes):

Mr Ramsey,
Listen carefully! We are a group of individuals that represent a small foreign

faction. We respect your bussiness but not the country that it serves. At this time we have your daughter in our posession. She is safe and unharmed and if you want her to see 1997, you must follow our instructions to the letter.

You will withdraw $118,000.00 from you account. $100,000 will be in $100 bills and the remaining $18,000 in $20 bills. Make sure that you bring an adequate size attaché to the bank. When you get home you will put the money in a brown paper bag. I will call you between 8 and 10am tomorrow to instruct you on delivery. The delivery will be exhausting so I advise you to be rested. If we monitor you getting the money early, we might call you early to arrange an earlier delivery of the money and hence a earlier pick-up of your daughter.

Any deviation of my instructions will result in the immediate execution of your daughter. You will also be denied her remains for proper burial. The two gentlemen watching over your daughter do not particularly like you so I advise you not to provoke them. Speaking to anyone about your situation, such as Police, FBI, etc., will result in your daughter being beheaded. If we catch you talking to a stray dog, she dies. If you alert bank authorities, she dies.

If the money is in any way marked or tampered with, she dies. You will be scanned for electronic devices and if any are found, she dies. You can try to deceive us but be warned that we are familiar with Law enforcement countermeasures and tactics. You stand a 99% chance of killing your daughter if you try to out smart us. Follow our instructions and you stand a 100% chance of getting her back. You and your family are under constant scrutiny as well as the authorities. Don't try to grow a brain John. You are not the only fat cat around so don't think that killing will be difficult. Don't underestimate us John. Use that good southern common sense of yours. It is up to you now John!

Victory!
SBTC

Millionaire businessman John Ramsey had moved his family and his computer firm, Access Graphics, to Boulder in 1991. Five years later, the company was booming and on 20 December 1996 celebrated its first billion-dollar year. But the celebrations were short-lived. Six days later, John Ramsey found his daughter's strangled body in the basement storeroom of his home, eight hours after she had been reported kidnapped.

In a television interview on 1 January 1997, Patsy

Ramsey described how she found the kidnappers' note. She said, 'I'd just gotten up. We were going visiting and it was quite early in the morning, and I had got dressed and was on my way to the kitchen to make some coffee, and we have a back staircase from the bedroom areas, and I always come down the staircase, and I am usually the first one down. The note was lying across the … three pages … across the run of one of the stair treads. It was kind of dimly lit.

'It was just very early in the morning, and I started to read it, and it was addressed to John. It said "Mr Ramsey" and it said, "we have your daughter". I don't know if I got any further than that. I immediately ran back upstairs and pushed open her door, and she was not in her bed, and I screamed for John.'

Asked how he came to look in the basement, John Ramsey told the newspaper interviewer, 'We'd waited until after the time that the call was supposed to have been made to us (by the kidnappers), and one of the detectives asked me and my friend who were there to go through every inch of the house to see if there was anything unusual or abnormal that looked out of place. Look for clues, asking us to do that, gave us something more to do to occupy our mind, and so we started in the basement, and … and we were just looking, and we … one room in the basement that … when I opened the door … there were no windows in that room, and I turned the light on, and I … that was her.'

ust after I retired from the Metropolitan Police in 1999 I received a telephone call from a man named Art Dworken. He introduced himself as Chief Crime Reporter of the *National Examiner*, the American newspaper based in Florida. Dworken began by telling me I was probably familiar with the JonBenet Ramsey case. Imagine my embarrassment when I had to tell him I hadn't heard of it! He asked me if I would give the case my time and consideration, but a bit defensively I asked him, 'Why should I?' I suppose I was a little guarded because the press have not always been kind to me. I just wanted to establish why a foreign journalist would want me to become involved in a case that had obviously attracted a great deal of attention in another country.

Anyway, I agreed to co-operate as far as I could, and later found out that a programme documenting the murder had actually been screened on British television. I told Art that if he would send me a picture of the victim, I would attempt to get information from my spirit helpers. Imagine my surprise when, a few days later, a postal delivery man knocked at my door carrying a large special delivery from Florida. Inside was a set of case papers, ranging from profiles of every witness and suspect, the victim's profile and pictures, autopsy report and ransom note. I was intrigued that so much detailed information was so readily available to the American press, something I'd not come across in my 30 years as a British police officer.

In some ways, I found this gluttony of information a distraction because, when working as a psychic, I prefer the minimal amount of information and rely on my spirit helpers to give me the clues.

I sat down and, for the first time ever, read all this information. In subdued lighting in my sitting room, I concentrated on the ransom note. I prayed to spirit and the following information was given to me.

The parents were not responsible for their daughter's death. But the murderer was someone known to Mr Ramsey, a man for whom the murderer would have considerable respect, such as an employee or a neighbour. This was why the ransom note was addressed to Mr Ramsey only. The note was not written by someone representing a group, as the impression had been given, but by an individual who did not act entirely alone.

I was very conscious that the person who wrote the ransom note, and the murderer, were one and the same. I could see that this person was familiar with the Ramseys' home and had been there prior to the killing. One other person knows the truth about the murder, a person who is very close to the murderer, although that person played no active part in the crime itself.

I saw the Ramseys' house as being large, with a grassed area at the rear, probably an open garden which dropped away. There was a large tree not too far from the kitchen door. I asked spirit the significance of showing me this particular area and I was told this was the route taken by the murderer who entered the house via the kitchen door (no force used), made his way through the house and down into the basement area via the rear stairs. The time of day was early evening and the ransom note had already been prepared and written. I saw this basement room as being a dirty, dingy room. I could see that the murderer waited in there prior to creeping stealthily to the little girl's bedroom and seizing her. Sadly, JonBenet was killed in that basement room almost as soon as she was seized and the ransom note was left by the killer as he fled the scene. The murderer's reason for doing this was to cause even more distress to her parents, especially her father. The killer was both besotted and jealous of the little girl and this was a totally needless crime.

The murderer likes a drink and would have to be aware that his drinking habits could get a bit out of hand. He has written the note with his unnatural hand (so if he was right-handed, he wrote it with his left hand). He is someone who is artistic and who has perhaps been involved in the entertainment field. This is a person who under-achieved educationally and who suffers with back problems. If that sounds a bit odd, it is the way this information has come to me.

I believe the police have already spoken to the murderer. I also believe this murder was committed because of jealousy — jealousy of the talented and beautiful little girl, and of her father, a wealthy and successful businessman.

•11•

Ring is the Key

Case History
The following crime report appeared in The Toronto
Star *in 1994: 'Finding an expensive ring taken from
an 80-year-old woman, murdered and sexually assaulted
earlier this summer, would provide a breakthrough in
the search for her killer, Metro police say.*

*'"The ring is the key," homicide Detective Tony Smith
said yesterday, commenting on the June 24 death of
Margaret McDonald, of Lascelles Blvd, in North York.
"Someone has it, or may have received it unwittingly,"'
Smith told the* Star *after a news conference.*

*The ring is "unique" and consists of an emerald
centre stone with two diamond guard stones. On both
sides of the emerald are outer bands with diamonds in
the centre and emeralds at the ends.*

Police believe a man, or men, broke into the woman's stately home by forcing a sliding door at the rear of the house. Her home — she lived alone — was ransacked. She died of head injuries and a slashed throat, police have confirmed. Smith said the ring is worth "thousands of dollars".'

Investigators checked pawn shops and jewellery distributors without success. It was established that Margaret McDonald died sometime between 12.30pm, when she spoke on the telephone, and 5.45pm when a friend knocked on her door and became worried because there was no answer. The woman's body was discovered in an upstairs bedroom by her 26-year-old granddaughter, Susan. She had been sexually assaulted and, apart from the ring, a number of other items were also missing, including a Swatch brand wristwatch, and a Vivitar TEC45 camera.

Police established that a knife and 'blunt object' had been used in the attack and that these had been recovered. It was believed the intruder, or intruders, entered the house through the back door.

The Toronto Chief of Police issued a poster offering a $100,000 reward for information leading to the arrest and conviction of Margaret McDonald's killers.

The poster carried the descriptions of three men seen in the area around the time of the murder. These descriptions were as follows:

1. Male, approximately 5 feet 10 inches tall, solid medium build, black hair pulled tightly

back into a pony tail which extends to the middle area of the shoulder blades, wearing black leather pants and black boots with large heels.

2. Male, white, mid 20s, between 5 feet 6 inches and 5 feet 7 inches tall, thin build, wearing a handkerchief or headband on his head, earring in his left ear, black leather jacket with silver studs, black leather pants and black boots.

3. Male, white, 19 to 23 years old, 6 feet 1 inches tall, slim build, clean shaven, long brown hair just past his shoulder, wearing a well-worn black leather jacket with silver buckles, possibly blue jeans with the knee torn out, carrying a school-type bag over his shoulder.

This was another Canadian job for me. From my home in Britain, in a telephone conversation with Mike King in Toronto, I made the following comments about the nature of this murder and the perpetrators of the crime, based on spirit information I received. I confirm that I had no prior knowledge of this case, other than the details given to me by King that an elderly woman had been found murdered in her home. That was it. The following are the notes taken by Mike King as I relayed the information over the telephone to him.

Time of 11.00am is critical. Does deceased woman's husband have a moustache? She was ill prior to murder and saw a doctor. She was an independent, rather stubborn woman.

I can see drainage work in area of murder scene prior to the murder. Month of May is critical. The woman was about 84. She had a ring with green stones specially made for her. She was incontinent at the time of her death. I see a person with the name Evelyn, or it may be Edith, involved. The dead woman was bludgeoned to death with blows across the back of her head. And she was stabbed.

Sexual assault followed the murder. The woman carried scented hankies. She was found in a double bed, lying on her right side. There was a small window to the right of her bed.

I see two men entering the dead woman's home from a rear door. One is dark-haired, with dark skin. The other is taller, and they are related. One has a pony tail hairstyle. I am getting the word 'Detroit'.

There is a car wash near the house and a white van was seen in the area. Perhaps one of the suspects played hockey. One of the two men placed his hand under the woman's bed ... was it checked for prints?

Woman has three daughters; one is very good in school. She could be a teacher. I see a grandson who is somehow involved. Was this a halal (Muslim) style killing?

The stolen ring has left the country; it was sold to a relative. There is a red tarmac drive outside the house.

I believe this murder was set up by somebody with a familiar knowledge of the old lady's home and her movements. They were aware of her possessions which I do not believe will be recovered. However, while DNA exists there is a good chance the murderers will be arrested.

·12·

Heaven on Earth

God is the creator of everything, absolutely everything. He is the boss. However, suggest this to scientists and most of them will be quick to disagree as though they know all the answers. They do not. Ask scientists to create a seed that will become a plant and they cannot do it. So they haven't got all the answers to life nor, for that matter, to death. Scientists, like many ordinary people, measure their beliefs against what they can actually see. If they cannot see it, touch it or prove it, then it cannot be possible.

Some people are like that with spiritualism. Until they receive a message, until it is proved to them to their satisfaction, they will not believe contact with spirit is possible. I am not saying this attitude is necessarily wrong, but when a person comes to one of my demonstrations, at least that person is opening up his or her mind to contact with spirit being possible. I am inviting these people to look at, and try to see, what I know does exist. If they will not even allow themselves to take a look, how can they possibly become aware? There is no need for me to cram my own awareness of life after death down their throats because I know people will quickly see it for themselves if they just give themselves the chance.

The American psychic investigator James Randi and Britain's own international magician Paul Daniels claim they can replicate anything a medium can do. All I would say is that magicians are very much in control of their own ability to create illusions or to perform trickery. They manipulate. But as a medium on a public stage, giving a demonstration, I cannot manipulate and I am certainly not in control of the situation, other than that I pass on messages which I receive from spirit. The only test of my ability is if the recipient, from his own knowledge of the spirit I am linked to, can relate to the information I pass on. If he cannot, then I am either a clever rogue or I have my lines crossed. I know I am not the former but, just occasionally, I might initially pass on messages to the wrong person. Then it is up to me to make sure I find the correct recipient by careful questioning — as I had to do as a police officer.

Why should anyone believe there is a God? Many of us don't get to meet the Queen, or even to see her, but we know she exists and we know she is within our reach if we go through the right channels. It is the same with God. I know He exists but I haven't met Him, not yet anyway. But I will eventually, perhaps not even on my next level of spiritual development, or even the one after that — but eventually. Will I recognise Him when I see Him? Is God black, white, yellow? Is God a man or a woman? Is He fat, or thin? Does He wear a gown, or jacket and trousers?

If you were to ask a classroom of children in Britain, Africa and China to draw a picture of God, they would show three different kinds of interpretations, but they would each show their own picture of what they believe God looks like. In the same way, if we were to draw a picture of ourselves without looking in a mirror, it is unlikely it would be a true representation. In the spirit world, the power of spirit allows us to imagine whatever shape we want to be.

In the film *Ghost* the separation of the physical and spiritual being was shown brilliantly. Terrible things happen to physical bodies. They become mutilated, drowned, beheaded, or can die of a heart-attack. Bodies can be eaten alive by disease before they die. What is certain is that, in the end, the physical body is discarded like an overcoat after it has served its purpose in our earthly life, allowing the spirit to cross into the spirit world which is all about us.

I try to explain this 'changeover' by describing how spirit goes to a recovery room, a kind of spirit world recuperation and reception area. Imagine the anguish of a spirit on its lonely travels in a completely new environment immediately after death. The spirit world eases the burden by ensuring the new spirit is met by the spirit of someone who was known to it on earth. Suddenly the shock of death turns into the joy, happiness and reassurance of a reunion with a friend or former loved one. The spirit recovery area is where we come to terms with death and our new life in spirit. I will probably meet my dear old granddad to whom I was especially close when he was alive. If I was to die now, he would probably be there to welcome me; or my departed son, Mathew, would greet me. Or both of them. That reunion could occur along the lines of: 'Hello, Keith. You have died and I am here to welcome you into your new life.'

'How did I die, Granddad?' I might well ask, because so often we either don't know we have died, or we haven't a clue how it happened, especially if it was traumatic. My granddad or my son would show me how I had died, so that I would understand and accept my fate.

If, in your physical life, you do not believe in life after death, you would not expect to find yourself in the spirit world. You would convince yourself there is no life after death because that is your conscious body speaking. Your spiritual being — that inner energy which is the real you — is well aware of there being life after death.

My granddad would then make it quite clear to me that I had died, that I was now in spirit. I would then meet up with departed family and friends, although people do not stay together in the spirit world any more than they do in the physical world. That this is the case saddens some people who like to think they will become united for ever with everyone they have lost on earth. Think of it this way: when I go to work in this life, I do not take my wife and children with me. I don't take my mum and dad, nor my aunt and uncle. We all lead separate lives, and we all learn separate lessons. This is why spirit spends time in the 'recovery area'. It is there that we renew old acquaintances. When we know they are fine and they know we are fine, everyone moves on. We are beginning to understand our spiritual consciousness and are coming to terms with life in this new world.

As a baby needs to be taught how to feed itself, how to walk and how to talk in order to fulfil its material needs, so our spirit needs to be taught how to function in the spirit world.

Sometimes I pick up the strong spirit of someone who has just passed over. That spirit still has strong earthly pulls; it will be desperate to reassure those it has left behind that it is in good shape, so to speak. In such a situation, I might say to my departed granddad, 'I just want to pop back and tell my wife that I am all right. I want my kids to know I am all right.'

If my will is strong enough, then I will do this. On earth, if your will and your beliefs are strong, you will want to contact your loved ones who have passed into spirit. They will be equally reassured that you have understood what has happened and that you are not grieving for them.

When I was at police training school, another recruit told me how he had woken in the early hours of one morning when his fiancée was due to fly back from a holiday in Spain. He could not sleep. That morning over breakfast his postman father made a cup of tea and handed it to his son. The young man dropped the cup, which smashed on the hard kitchen floor. 'Oh, my God. Mary is dead!' he had shouted despairingly.

His father asked why Mary should be dead, adding, 'Besides, she can't be. She doesn't even fly until nine.'

They both later learned that Mary had taken an earlier flight and the plane had crashed, killing everyone on board.

The incident was one that many people will

have experienced. At the moment my police cadet pal dropped his cup of tea, he had been 'touched' by the spirit of his fiancée, Mary, at the very moment she died in the plane crash. Her spirit was saying 'goodbye' in an attempt to reassure a loved one that her spirit lived on in another dimension.

It is natural for all of us to be curious about life after death, to want to know what life is like in the spirit world. I am often asked, and all I can really do is give an idea based on accounts given to me and other clairvoyants by spirit.

As a child, I believed that Heaven was above and beyond the clouds; I thought that people who had died actually walked around on clouds. It was a kid's view of Heaven. But once you have flown in an aeroplane, that illusion is quickly shattered.

Ask 50 clairvoyants to describe Heaven and they will each have different descriptions. It is hardly surprising because they haven't been there! Some more spiritually developed mediums have visions. My own visions of life in the spirit world show a world without houses, no cars, no traffic problems other than the spiritual traffic of many people doing what they do.

When we get to the spirit world, we don't know what to expect or what we will look like. If I said to you, as from 2.00pm today, you will be in Heaven, how could you possible know what to expect? How would you know what to expect to look like one minute past two? Equally, we wouldn't know what was expected of us. I believe we will be what we want to be, and will take on the shape most familiar to us, with just a few amendments. If I want to be slimmer, I will be slimmer. Those who want to be a bit younger can be a bit younger. So, over there, you are what you want to be. And although this is not a solid form, you take on a shape that is more a transparency of your physical. We take on an intangible shape, which is probably what people 'see' when they see a ghost. The energy that spirit creates to come back and make itself visible is only a form which spirit knows will be recognisable to those who are alive. Perhaps an easier way to understand how spirits probably 'see' themselves and others is to think of someone you know well and conjure up his or her image in your mind's eye. The image represents the way a spirit would look.

So, for the first period in the spirit world we are this transparency. We do exist there in a kind of spiritual solidity, but not a physical one. We have left the physical part of our being behind, and if the manner of that departure has not totally ruined our body (perhaps through being burned or mutilation, for example) then those we leave behind make sure our body is of no further use to us or anyone else by cremating or burying it. Our spirit, the real energy which is us, has long gone. If the body we leave behind at death is empty because spirit has vacated it, then why not put the remaining bits to good use? Let the man next door, who is going blind, have my eyes; allow a surgeon to take out my heart and give it to someone whose life it might extend, or improve. These organs are of no further use to me when I have died. We do this with cars, so we should think of death as a kind of breaker's yard for our bodies. Spirit is the life force and our bodies cannot function without it. A scientist will say that a body cannot function without a heart so, when that packs up, the body dies. When physical life is no longer sustainable, the spirit moves on.

The first stage of spirit life is like a holiday, but a holiday that is not measured by time because there is no time in the spirit world. No clocks, no watches. Time is man-made, not something created by God. We arrive in Heaven with memories of the physical world but without any physical disabilities. If I was legless when I was alive, I could have my legs back in spirit if I wanted them, albeit as a part of the 'spirit transparency' I was telling you about. Interestingly, this is why psychic artists will often draw a picture of a spirit person at an age in their mortal life when they liked themselves best.

I am told by spirit there are halls of learning over there. Does this mean centres like universities? Probably not, but 'learning centres' where lesser developed spirits can be helped to progress.

Keith Charles

I am often asked, 'When I die, will I meet up
with the child I lost?' The answer is 'Yes'. Families
meet up whether there are three husbands or six
wives, yet there is no worldly animosity, no
bitterness, no pain, just unrestricted joy. You meet
up, and move on. If I had murdered my wife on
earth and later died, we would meet up in spirit
but there would be no bitterness, no hate, no
jealousy. These are all human emotions which we
leave behind. Only the all-embracing feeling of
love exists in spirit. This is where the so-called
halls of learning, as I like to call them, come into
their own. Murderers are taught that the taking
of another life is not tolerated. It is a kind of
spiritual cleansing process, a learning that is going
on all the time. Spirit needs to be taught, just as
humans do. That is why I tell people, with half a
smile, that they do not die and suddenly sprout
wings, or become angels overnight. Just because
they are dead, it does not give them a passport to
holiness. We take our experiences, our earthly
misdeeds, with us, which is why there is a need in
spirit for the learning centres.

What about reincarnation? Do people die, go
into spirit then return to human life again? From
the teachings I have received from spirit guides,
there is reincarnation for some. Reincarnation is
the return of a spiritual life from Heaven back
into an earth life. It happens to those who have
missed out on particular lessons in this life. It is,

perhaps, a bit like being downgraded at school. A pupil needs to go back to a lower class to go over and pick up on lessons they haven't yet absorbed.

I do not believe that life on earth is the inception of spirit. We are spirit before we come to earth, so, unless we are reincarnated spirit, we are new to this earth. I don't want mothers panicking, thinking their babies are reincarnated spirits. It is possible, but unlikely. There is also a good chance that on earth we sometimes carry student spirits needing to learn lessons that we on earth may be learning. The spirit attaches itself to us and shadows us, though we wouldn't know this was happening.

Let us look at stress. Suppose I am going through an especially stressful time and a spirit I will call 'Mr X' happens to need to learn how to cope with the same kind of stress which caused him to take his own life by suicide. Mr X walks with me, and learns. He may be with me for a day, a month, a year — in earth time — the duration doesn't matter. Only a psychic might sense that this was happening. Mr X then moves on in his spiritual development, having learned how he should have coped with physical stress. These views are not necessarily held by all spiritualists or clairvoyants but they are responses from spirit to questions put to me. I have asked spirit guides for these answers.

Heaven is all around us. It is not a separate

place, above the clouds for example, or on another planet. The spirit world is in a different dimension, but still where we are. That is why I can tell someone at one of my meetings, 'This morning at eight you put on a pair of brown shoes, but suddenly changed your mind and wore black shoes instead. I know this because your dad, in spirit, is telling me he saw you.' That spirit father has got to be in this world to see it happen.

Everybody knows what a television does, and that to make it work it is necessary to push the button to the 'on' position. If my dead granddad wants to see how I am getting on, he has to push his 'on' button to look into my world. If he feels he needs to influence me in some way, then he will do so. Call it psychic, call it instinct, but most of us have experienced this kind of help at one time or another, help which has probably come from spirit.

Sometimes my views on life after death are considered controversial, but this doesn't necessarily make them wrong. There was one occasion when this wasn't good enough for a certain lady at one of my meetings in the City Hall, Sheffield. She wanted to know what happened to babies when they go to the spirit world. When I told her they grow up and develop spiritually, this woman asked, 'So you disagree with Doris Stokes?' I told her that I had no idea of Doris Stokes's views on the matter. She said she had read in one of Doris's books that children who die are kept in capsules waiting for their mothers to join them in the spirit world. I had to tell the lady that if that was Doris Stokes's explanation, I totally disagreed. Then came the cruncher. The woman remarked, 'Well, you are wrong because Doris Stokes said so!'

The idea that a baby dies and is put in a capsule until its mother joins it in spirit, perhaps 60 years later, is totally unacceptable to me. It would also be totally selfish and I do not believe spirit works that way. I believe Doris was wrong to say that it does.

Clairvoyants, spiritualists and mediums do not always agree. How much that was said and written about Jesus was true? Probably less than 10 per cent. The kind of miracles Jesus performed would now be taken more for granted and yet I have no doubts that He was a very highly evolved spirit who came to earth to bring people together.

I believe that Winston Churchill, who has communicated with us since his earthly death, did much the same thing but we never hailed him as the Son of God, although he saved Britain and Europe from the tyranny of Hitler. If Churchill had been given the same credence as Jesus, I see no reason why he would not have been upheld as another Messiah. I am not trying to compare Churchill with Jesus, but to emphasise the image we humans create, to show how powerful this can be to those under this influence.

We do not put many humans closer to God in our earthly system than the Pope, and yet nobody calls him the Son of God or claims that his spirit has descended from Heaven to save us all. Our intelligence and awareness are now so much more heightened than they were 2,000 years ago. Fewer people now accept religion parrot fashion. They want a lot more from religion, that is why they are now looking more to spiritualism with their questions about life and death. People are inquisitive, prepared to question their own faith and the faith of others in the relentless search to find the truth. Those who fear this search will throw up their red herrings in an effort to discredit those seeking the truth. Of course, they will not succeed.

Ask many people what spiritualism conjures up in their minds and they will probably tell you it is of a group of little old ladies sitting round a table in a darkened room, fingers touching, with the medium calling out in a droning, emotionless voice, 'Is there anyone there wanting to talk to us?'

Summoning up the spirit world in this manner has been most people's idea of spiritualism since it became the object of increased public curiosity in the late 1940s. Blame the likes of that larger-than-life actress Margaret Rutherford as Madame Arcati in such films as *Blithe Spirit*. When she went into a trance and brought 'the other world' into her living room, all kinds of weird and wonderful things happened, most of them hilarious, most of them portrayed as trickery, and all of them under the label of entertainment. It was therefore hardly surprising that few people at that time took Madam Arcati, her little old ladies and spiritualism too seriously.

Unfortunately, this imagery still lingers on because the followers of spiritualism and those who seek the truth about life after death, have largely failed to catapult themselves into the twenty-first century with any conviction. It is my intention, as one of spiritualism's younger — and probably more outspoken — followers to play my part in spreading greater understanding about the truth and effectiveness of mediumship.

The Madam Arcatis are still around and you can spot their tiny advertisements in the personal columns of many local newspapers, even on the Internet, but they should be seen more for their entertainment value than their psychic intuition. I just wish these fringe psychics would stop giving genuine, practising mediums a bad name. It is difficult enough that we cannot seem to cast off the boring, dowdy, old-fashioned reputation without having every Tom, Dick and Harriet calling themselves psychic astrologers and tarnishing our image still further.

Elderly women, gypsy scarves on their heads,

who sit on piers reading tea leaves, Tarot cards and palms, are seldom genuinely gifted mediums, however much they may advertise themselves as such, or tell their clients. They have developed a nice line in patter which gives the punter a ray of hope, usually about love, money and work. It is seldom worth the £10 to £30, or more, they charge.

Even the media tends to regard us as freaks who have crawled out of the woodwork. They come to us around Hallowe'en and beg us to go on television to take part in chat shows, only to spend the interview questioning our sincerity and ability. I would be a rich man if I had a pound every time I have been asked, 'Can you prove it is possible to contact the dead?'

My answer is always, 'Can you prove that I cannot?'

I have had many experiences and much evidence to satisfy me that there is a spirit link between this world and the next but when the issues get aired on television, the tests are seldom fair. Sadly, I have to say I don't think they are intended to be; they are discussed for their entertainment value, not to find evidence that will uphold them. I am happy to appear on television shows to talk about clairvoyance, and I have done so on numerous occasions, but I have always made sure I was in control of what I was expected to do, or discuss. If I've ever felt this control slipping away from me, then I have quickly regained it.

Personally, I prefer presenting or taking part in radio phone-in programmes. These have included shows for Radio One, Southern Sound, Norwich Radio, Radio Leeds and Capital Radio. I have had very few trouble-makers. Sometimes, though, the trouble comes from within, as was the case when I made a guest appearance on the BBC's local radio station in Exeter. The DJ handling the interview was all charm when I arrived at the station. He told me we were going to have a really smashing afternoon and have lots of fun with the listeners. I was encouraged to 'make myself at home' in the big studio. Then he went on air.

'Today, I've got with me Keith Charles, the psychic policeman. He is appearing at St George's Hall, in Exeter,' he told his listeners. Then came the bombshell, 'Now then, Keith, tell me, what is your view on the Immaculate Conception?' He then leapt out of his seat, walked across the studio and began sorting out records, leaving me to answer a question that had very little relevance to clairvoyance! Plunged into an impossible situation over which I could so easily have lost total control, I was most uncomfortable for about ten minutes. I knew I had to fight back or I would have had little credibility left with the people of Exeter. I gave my view about the Immaculate Conception for what it was worth, and when the DJ told me I'd probably just offended every Catholic in the country, I added, 'Sorry, but you asked me along to give my opinions. That is my opinion. If it doesn't fall in line with what you would have liked me to say, that is your problem. Not mine! Perhaps you should have asked me a more relevant question!'

Looking back, with the experience I have now gained, I would now have no hesitation explaining to the listeners exactly what that DJ was doing, not bothering to answer the question, leaving him to scramble back to his microphone!

Controversy, of course, can help raise the profile of an issue so I consider it productive arguing my own belief that there is life after death, and listening to the arguments of those who believe there is not. When the film *Ghost* hit the big screen, I didn't give it much thought because I am not much of a cinemagoer. Then a friend told me the film was about a clairvoyant and that I should see it, so I took an evening off to see the film, starring Patrick Swayze. I was not disappointed. Off-screen, Swayze related what he called a personal spiritual experience, revealing that at one point in his life a surfing accident left him on the verge of drowning. He thought he was a goner when, suddenly, an ancient warrior brandishing a sword in his right hand and covered in body paint, rose up out of the water in front of him. Swayze said, 'He just grabbed hold of me, told me not to panic and reassured me we would make it to safety — which we did.'

Of course, this could have been a publicity story to push the film, but I tend to think not. More likely the warrior was Patrick's own spirit guide who came to his rescue in response to the actor's psychic call for help. My own 'doorman', as we call our guides, is a Mongolian warrior, so we have something in common! *Ghost* did a great deal to stimulate interest in the question of life after death, and Patrick Swayze's personal experience gave many people a lot to think about. If people are thinking seriously about such issues, they are more likely to draw their own favourable conclusions.

Happily, when journalist Anne Barrowclough came to interview me for a newspaper article, she was able to draw her own conclusions from things I was able to tell her about her grandfather that nobody outside her family could have known — other than spirit. Though, to begin with, she thought I'd got things wrong.

She wrote in her story, 'Detective Keith Charles had been checking up on me before I arrived at his neat house in the London suburbs. He hadn't been speaking to my friends, but doing something which is equally natural to him. Talking to the spirit world.'

After I'd welcomed Anne to my home, made

her a cup of tea and settled her in, I began talking to her, rather than the other way round. I told her, 'Barrowclough was not your real name. Your father's father was called both William and Henry.' I also said she had joined her newspaper only within the past six months and that I had been informed by spirit that she would turn up at my house in a red skirt, black top and wearing a pendant.

'I was, in fact, wearing a tan and beige outfit,' wrote Anne. 'However, not only was everything else correct, but some of the facts are known only to members of my family who live in Australia.

'At first, we argued about my father's father. I insisted his name was William and there was no Henry.

'"Yes, there is," said Keith. "The name of your father's father is William and Henry." Then I realised he was right. William Jamieson, my grandfather, faked his suicide and abandoned the family when my father was a toddler. For the next five years, Uncle Henry, my grandmother's brother, brought my father up while my grandmother traipsed around England searching for her husband. My father told me the story only this year, saying, "I regarded Uncle Henry as my real dad." Keith just shrugged as I told him. "Well, I knew it was Henry because he's with us now, and telling me all this," added Keith. He described him — correctly — as a big, burly chap, adding, "Henry is your guardian angel."

'Even to the most sceptical, this kind of "reading" can be persuasive. It's even more so when done in Keith's matter-of-fact way,' concluded Anne.

•13•

Psychic to the Stars

Sir Elton John and Sir Paul McCartney probably do not know it and may not even want to know it, but in terms of their spiritual energy they are both psychic superstars. I see this aura of powerful spiritual energy which surrounds them like a snug-fitting, misty overcoat. As a developed clairvoyant, if I stood alongside either of them I would feel the glow that comes from contact with the energy of very special souls like these. They are outstanding musicians who would make equally gifted healers, and yet they are probably totally unaware of this 'power' within them.

I would like to ask them if they are aware that people are drawn towards them, not so much because they are famous but because they have what we tend to call 'magnetic personalities'? Have they noticed how children, in particular, have an irresistible urge to stand close? This happens with psychically developed people, although this ability to 'attract' others is seldom understood for what it often is — a strong psychic aura.

In the memorable words of actor Clint Eastwood, as Dirty Harry, it would 'make my day' to have a little time in the company of Elton and Paul to explore their undoubted spiritual gift. It is interesting to me that great musicians are often imbued with psychic powers, but are they good musicians because of this spirituality, or are they spiritual because they are great musicians? It's not a question I can answer, as yet.

Two other stars of the rock and pop world with interesting psychic stories to tell are Jet Harris, formerly of The Shadows, the group which helped Cliff Richard to international stardom, and Ricky Valance, singing star of the Sixties whose recording 'Tell Laura I Love Her' was a chart-topper.

It is probably best that both Jet and Ricky tell their own fascinating stories of how spiritualism changed their lives for the better.

Psychic Detective

Jet Harris

'It was a friend of a friend of Keith Charles who first invited me to one of Keith's psychic evenings. I can't remember the precise location, other than that it was in London, but I do recall that I was quite overwhelmed by the wonderfully happy and spiritual people I met there. They even presented me with a little gift of African oak, carved as clasped hands. I was told that if I rubbed those "hands" whenever I felt a bit tense, the stress would drain away.

'I suppose I went to this meeting because I had a long-standing interest in spiritualism. I once read a book written by a priest who claimed he was in touch with the spirit of a dead priest. The latter described what life was like in the spirit world and this fascinated me, so when Keith's invitation came along it seemed a good opportunity to revive my curiosity about life after death.

'According to the spirit priest, everybody in the spirit world is about 30 years of age, everyone dresses the same and there is no sex over there. I particularly liked the flowery stuff in his book where it said that in Heaven when you pick up a handful of sand and let it fall through your fingers, it makes a tuneful, tinkling sound. The grass tinkles, too, when you walk over it. There are no such things as sick people, sick flowers, or sick anything. Life there is perfection. People can study whatever they want and there is so much to do, including shows and concerts; I liked that because it means I will be able to carry on being a musician or a photographer, which is another big interest and pleasure of mine.

'We all have to believe in something, so I now believe this is our fate when we leave this life. I definitely feel I am psychic because I have strong feelings about things, which is what intuition is all about, I suppose. Keith especially impressed me because he told me he could see me in a big show. I told him I'd been in big shows with The Shadows, but that was well in the past.

' "No, I see you in another big show with The Shadows."

'At the time, that didn't seem at all likely. Some months later, though, right out of the blue, I did get to play again with The Shadows and Cliff Richard, at Wembley Stadium. That hadn't even been planned when I spoke to Keith.'

Ricky Valance

'Keith put me in touch with my dead father and came up with some quite astounding facts with regard to him; facts only I could have known. We met in my dressing room when I was on a concert tour. I was very into spiritualism and that kind of thing, so I asked Keith to give me a reading. He told me there was the spirit of a gentleman in the room with us and he went on to describe my father who died about eight years before. What shook me was the kind of detail he was able to produce, such as the fact that my father had been very ill with a chest problem which caused his chest to cave in. He was right. My father suffered from spondylitis (inflammation of the vertebrae), so he hit the nail right on the head. Nobody could have known that, other than me.

'Keith then went on to say that my father knew I had been trying to contact him and that I was constantly thinking of him. Through Keith, my father reassured me that he was with me in spirit most of the time and that many of the ideas which came to me were put into my mind by my departed dad. Then came a touch of my father's typical sense of humour; he added that he became very frustrated when I didn't act on his advice!

'When Keith told me this gentleman kept calling me "boy", I knew it had to be my dad. It was him to a "T". He was an old Welshman — we're all Welsh — and he would often say to me, "Come on, boy," or "How are you, boy?" Keith told me I was not to worry any more about his fate because his spirit was very much alive and well on the other side. Keith said he had a stick which he used to carry in this life, and which he now carries with him in spirit. Then Keith asked me if my father had a dog in his earth life. No, he didn't, but he was very keen on animals, especially dogs. It seems he is now surrounded by them.

'I have to admit that I cried with the emotion of finally being convinced that I will meet my father again. I've always believed in a life after death, but now I have had proof enough for me that it isn't the end of the line when we die. It has alleviated a lot of my worries and given me a great deal of comfort.

'Maybe it is no coincidence that I have always felt that my life has been protected; just as well, really, because I have had many brushes with death. I have escaped two serious road crashes and a near-drowning incident which happened off Singapore. Even the song "Tell Laura I Love Her" was to do with death, about a guy who got killed in a stock car race, but it didn't glorify death. For me, its appeal was that it had such a lovely melody. Now I know that when I need to do so, I can probably contact my father again. That is comforting.'

I hope these two testimonies speak for themselves. Both Jet and Ricky stress the comfort they now enjoy from the proof they have had about the existence of life after death. As Ricky put it, 'This is not the end of the line.'

Many actors are also clairvoyant, so maybe it has something to do with artistic sensitivity. Television soap star William Roache, who was in the very first episode of *Coronation Street*, is another psychic sizzler and, for me, a special one because he knows the gift must be taken seriously. I have had the pleasure of meeting Bill a number of times and I have enjoyed some interesting chats with him about life after death along the lines of how serious-minded people can sensibly explore what is ahead of all of us when we die.

Bill was long-suffering schoolmaster Ken Barlow in *Coronation Street* when he invited me to Granada Studios, in Manchester, to talk about life after death, and to give him a psychic reading. We sat in the relative privacy of his dressing room, surrounded by mirrors, bathed in bright lights and the smell of make-up. It struck me at the time as a strange place to be talking about where we go when we die. But Bill has a very distinctive sense of humour and a belief in spirit life based on very personal experiences, so he wouldn't have cared where he discussed such matters as long as they were discussed seriously and sensibly. We did just that. In fact, I was flattered that he thought it would make good television to explore seriously the ability of a proven clairvoyant and the

implications of life after death. He said he would
want to take part in such a discussion and I told
him I would happily be his psychic guinea pig if
the idea could be taken forward!

I told Bill he would make a good medium, that
he is very spiritually aware but, as far as I know,
he has not even been to a psychic meeting. It is
possible that it's his star status which prevents him
from taking a more active interest, and I can
understand that. Imagine what would happen if
the press got to hear that he was at one of my
meetings in Manchester; they'd be cooking up all
kinds of stories! He prefers to conduct his private
life in private. However, Bill has spoken openly
about the grief he and his wife, Sara, experienced
when their 19-month-old baby daughter, Edwina,
died from bronchitis. In fact, at one point when
considering my involvement with Bill, I had a
vision of Edwina. I could see a little girl and I
sensed very strongly that when she was prepared
for her funeral a cross was placed in her right
hand, although I could not be sure who put it
there. Bill later said he was unaware of this
having happened, so a cross was not placed there
by Bill or Sara. Was I wrong? Or, if Edwina's
mother and father did not place a cross in her
little hand, maybe it was another member of the
family, or someone else? I have to say though,
that I am seldom wrong when I receive such
powerful visions, as this was.

Bill and Sara grieved very deeply over their loss of Edwina, to the point where they felt they might not even be able to cope with the final farewell to their daughter. On the morning of the funeral, Bill had a vision of his own when the spirit of baby Edwina came to him within a spiritual bright light which shone from one corner of his bedroom. Though she was so young, this was Edwina's way of saying to her mother and father, 'Stop grieving for me. I am happy. There is life after death.' Comforted by this experience, Bill and Sara were then able to handle the funeral, especially sad when it is that of a child.

'After the vision, I felt a great relief flood over me, and from that moment Sara and I began to rebuild our lives,' Bill later commented.

The actor, whose claim that he is the world's longest-serving soap actor has never been challenged, accepts that he is intuitive and psychic, but he has reservations about dabbling in the spirit world. He puts it this way: 'I've studied these things and know there are entities floating around in the ether looking for entry to our world. The trouble with spiritualism is that it opens up to these entities, and some of them aren't benign. You have to be very wary. We're not meant to be working in these area, but the time is coming when serious studies are going to be made, and when that happens I will be happy to come forward and work with serious people like Keith Charles. He has impressed me, and I know he is a sincere person. I have met some clairvoyants who are quacks and hoaxers. Unfortunately, the genuine ones, like Keith, are few in number.'

Regrettably, few people are as aware as Bill Roache about the need to take spiritualism seriously and that they should not treat it as a party trick, using the dangerous ouija board as a 'key' to open the door to the spirit world. It is all too easy to disturb the mischievous entities which Bill mentions. To help people understand what I mean by this, I say to them, 'You would not leave your front door open, would you? All right, a nice man might walk by and pop his head inside to tell you your front had been left open. But another man might also take advantage of an open front door, let himself in and cause a lot of bother!'

It is no different when I make contact with the spirit world. I have no idea what kind of spirit is going to come along, and when one does I make quite sure it is not intent on making mischief!

Singer Lulu came to a meeting, not so much because she was in need of spiritual comfort but, I would imagine, more out of curiosity. There was nothing wrong with that. Her husband John and their son came, too. The evening starred Doris Collins and was being filmed for Australian television, so Lulu's presence and that of several other showbusiness celebrities added a touch of glamour to the occasion.

Afterwards, over a cup of tea and biscuits, Lulu said to me, 'Doris is good, isn't she?' Then she asked what I did. I said I was also a medium. At this point, Lulu was invited to have her picture taken, and duly obliged, but Doris Collins appeared to be a little put out. She later complained to me that she did not think it was right to ask guest celebrities to pose for pictures. It was taking advantage of their visit. However, the cameras were rolling for the Australian television documentary and Doris Collins was the psychic star turn so perhaps she had some excuse for showing a little artistic temperament!

Lulu is another artiste with a definite gift of healing. It shows in her spiritual aura of mauve and pink. A lot of healing power comes from her and I would say that underneath that cool, bubbly, personality is a person who cares very deeply for the world's problems. She will care about homeless people. Perhaps she will care that she could also be a healer and consider developing her gift.

I came across blonde actress Kitty Aldridge when I was making house-to-house enquiries as a police officer. I knocked on her front door without knowing who was inside, or the name of the lady who opened it. What I can say is that as soon as I saw her, I knew we were going to get along well. She had a brilliant aura and showed herself to be a shrewd businesswoman with very strong motivation and sense of purpose. During our conversation on her doorstep, I happened to mention that I was a medium.

'Oh, come on in. My husband would love to have a chat with you,' she said excitedly.

I completed my police work with Kitty (star of the former television series *Paradise Club*) and her equally well-known film producer husband, Neil, then we all talked about life after death. They seemed fascinated that I was a psychic policeman.

Over the next few weeks and months, I spent quite a lot of time with Kitty and Neil. Neil also introduced me to his brother, Cedric, who had produced the American *Ninja Turtle* film. It's funny how things turn out through friendship, but in our case it blossomed to such an extent that we all chipped in to buy a greyhound. We called her Wolf Power, and raced her. She didn't make us much money but she won enough to pay for her keep. In fact, she was a finalist in three major races.

Kitty would make a good spiritual counsellor. I don't really think it is something she would want to do seriously, but she is a great listener to other people's problems. Both Kitty and Neil came to one of my psychic meetings in Chatham, Kent, out of curiosity. They told me they were very impressed with the large number of people there at a psychic meeting for the first time, as well as the large number of young people present. Kitty also presented a cheque to a young lad who had cancer.

Since that time, Kitty and Neil have gone their separate ways, as sometimes happens in life. I understand she is now very happy with Mark Knopfler of Dire Straits, and they have a daughter.

I have met a number of celebrities, a good few with psychic leanings. I have appeared with Richard and Judy on their morning show, on *The Big Breakfast*, Sky Sports, and others. But where Richard and Judy are concerned, I have noticed they have become more interested in psychic and spiritual matters. Johnny Vaughan and Lisa Tarbuck, of *The Big Breakfast*, are definitely intrigued by spiritual matters and Lisa has definite healing abilities. I have been in the company of Darren Day and Martine McCutcheon and they both have strong psychic intuition. I feel sure they must have had psychic experiences.

I was a guest on *The Lowri Turner Show* at BBC Television Centre, in Shepherd's Bush, to discuss spiritual healing along with the three main guests — Glen Hoddle, the former England manager, healer Eileen Drewery and a GP whose name I do not recall. It was an interesting experience.

On one of Esther Rantzen's shows, I found myself sitting next to actor Brian Blessed in the make-up room. He turned to me and said in his booming voice, 'What do you do then?'

I told him I was both a policeman and a medium.

'That's absolutely fascinating,' he replied and then spent several minutes questioning me (which I suppose was a bit of a role reversal). We had quite a deep conversation. It didn't surprise me that I was able to pick up from his vibrant aura that he was a very spiritual man who has experienced psychic phenomena first-hand. A man with a strong sense of fair play, strong-willed with more than a hint of stubbornness, both independent and intelligent, as well as a born leader. He is good at managing money and certainly enjoys a challenge, whether it is in his professional or personal life.

•14•

Questions You Ask

What do spirits do in Heaven? If it is the Paradise we have been told it is, do we spend our time there on hot, sandy beaches, without a care in the world (the spirit world, of course)? And when we die, do we meet angels? Do we even become one? Is there jealousy in Heaven? Will we meet God?

There are so many questions most of us have asked, or wanted to ask, about life after death. In the course of my many successful British tours, bringing clairvoyance to the man in the street, I have been asked just about every question there is to ask about spirit lives, so I thought it was time I did my best to try and provide some of the answers. By linking with my guide, Tobias, who gives me this insight, I hope many of you will find the answers to your own questions, and a good few more.

Can anyone be a medium?
In one word — no. The gift of mediumship is a gift from God along with the responsibility that goes with it. That you have this gift may not be apparent to you immediately, even though you may have many 'minor' experiences throughout your life until the gift reveals itself to you.

Is it wrong to contact the dead?
This is a question often asked by those who have been brought up with a strong religious background; a belief often nurtured by ignorance and fear. Spiritualism, as it is recognised today, began in 1848. Since that time there has been an avalanche of evidence constantly given to mediums by those communicators now in Heaven, showing conclusively that the so-called 'dead' lead a very active and productive life in their new spiritual home. They want to contact the loved ones they have left behind to prove their spiritual survival, but here on earth you can choose whether or not you want to receive that communication. The choice is yours.

Psychic Detective

How do I know if I am a medium?
You will know. You may see ghosts, feel a presence, or be especially sensitive to people and places. You may find you are able to 'know' things about people, in particular details of their family and friends who have passed away. You may find that when you visit places they have a presence which you can tune in to. Until you recognise that you have this gift, and you develop it under expert guidance, these experiences may even be a little disturbing. When it is developed, mediumship is a powerful ally.

How would I develop my gift?
You would need to find a good teacher through recommendation, or word of mouth, by pupils who have studied with, and been trained by, a reputable medium. Or you can go to your nearest spiritualist church and ask if they have a 'development circle'. If you don't know a local centre, you can write to the two main bodies in spiritualism: Greater World Christian Spiritualist Association, 3–5 Conway Street, London W1P 5HA; or the Spiritualists' National Union, Stansted Hall, Stansted, Essex CM24 8UD. If you are interested in contacting me, please write to: Keith Charles, Wimbledon Spiritualist Church, 136 Hartfield Road, Wimbledon, London SW19 3TJ.

Keith Charles

How do you see spirit?
When I am linked to my spirit guides, the person communicating with me may do so in various ways. In physical terms we have six senses and the communicator may use any or all of these senses to increase my ability to tune in with them. I have the gifts of 'clairvoyance', 'clairaudience' and 'clairsentience'. In simple terms, this means 'clear seeing', 'clear hearing' and 'clear smell'. So I may physically see, hear and smell the communicator. Sometimes, depending on whether or not the communicator is experienced, my view of them might be as a quite solid form, as clear as someone standing in front of me. Sometimes I will see the communicator just a little more clearly than a photographic transparency.

How do you 'hear' spirit?
When I hear a communicator, it comes to me as a tone of voice, perhaps gruff, deep, high-pitched, educated, a noticeable laugh, with an accent. I am also aware when a communicator has lost the power of speech in his earthly life; perhaps through illness or accident. And what about young children who die even before they have learned to speak? They can still communicate. Either they have grown in spirit since their passing, or I rely on them being accompanied in spirit by an adult communicator. Failing this, I rely on my own spirit guides to relay the messages

to me. The 'voice' of the communicator comes directly into my head, to a point just behind my ears.

How do you use your sense of smell?
I am often aware of smells that communicators impart to me which the message recipient may associate with a loved one who has passed over. It could be a particular perfume, fragrance or after-shave especially identifiable to the message receiver. On occasions, it is not necessarily a pleasant smell that comes to me. In the case of a spirit who had been a heavy smoker in his earthly life, I might well pick up the heavy smell of cigarette smoke. Thankfully, I've not yet had a communication from a spirit who worked in a fish factory!

What happens when you die?
We know that our spiritual body is 'housed' within our physical body. Most people understand that this is called the 'spirit' or 'soul'. The spirit cannot be seen as a living organ within the body, in the way that the heart, liver or brain, for example, can be seen, but it is still there. The spirit contains all a person's knowledge and personality along with the lessons and experiences learned in the earthly lifetime.

Think of the body as an overcoat. We use it, look after it and care for it until its purpose and use are finished. When we no longer have a need for it, we discard it. When our life has run its course on earth and the time has come for our spirit to leave and 'go home to Heaven', it does so unhindered or encumbered by whatever the cause of passing.

Is death painful?
On earth we are conditioned to feeling pain. It is a part of being physical. But at the time of passing there is no feeling of pain. Our spiritual leaves our physical body and with the life force gone, we escape all pain.

Who meets you when you pass over to spirit?
At the time of death, the physical body and the spiritual body separate, and the spirit is accompanied by that person's spiritual guide, or a formerly departed loved one, on its journey to Heaven. A 'near-death experience' (NDE) is when someone dies and subsequently comes back to life again. They often describe going through a tunnel and seeing a beautiful light and colours, and being met by a dead loved one. The majority of witnesses say they did not want to return to their earth life, but were instructed to do so. Such experiences seem to reassure people and they no longer have a fear of crossing over.

Author Jilly Cooper tells a story concerning a good friend of hers who had allegedly experienced the 'crossing over' in a near-death experience. This friend had died clinically during an operation and went to 'a place with this divinely wonderful light, happy people and an angel'. She had wanted to enter this beautiful place, but the angel refused her entry, explaining that there were people on earth who still needed her to be there.

What people are experiencing here is a glimpse into Heaven. Non-believers and some scientists would try to explain this by saying that the mind creates illusions brought on by physical and chemical changes in the body at, or near, death. However, research carried out by a Southampton doctor has probably established beyond doubt that the alleged chemicals responsible for these 'illusions' are not physically produced by the body at death.

What is it like in Heaven?
Heaven is all around us. It is in a different dimension, but it is still there. When we die, there are several stages of progression to our destination in the spirit world. Let us take a look at these stages, and the first is Arriving in Heaven. The physical body has gone and you can now look like whatever you want! The spirit form is something like a photographic transparency. The new spirit body is restored to full health and there is a new feeling of freedom and power. But

don't get carried away with the idea that this is like some 'free ticket' to paradise! There are disciplines, along with instruction and teachings in spiritual development. There is even help and instruction given on how to communicate with those loved ones left behind. It is at this early stage that people may choose to work with animals or children. Or something else that interests them. At this stage, all is possible.

The tranquillity of Heaven, the peace, the love and the deep sense of being and belonging is what touches the new spirit most when it arrives in Heaven.

What do we look like in Heaven?
We spend our earth lives preoccupied with our looks. Am I too fat? Too thin? Too short? Too tall? Do I look old? Every time we leave our front doors we are conscious of our looks, so it stands to reason that we should want to know what we look like in Heaven. But this is a difficult question to answer because we are short of the spiritually developed vision they have there.

What I do know is that earthly deformities and disabilities are not carried forward. A blind person is not blind in Heaven. All our physical disabilities or restrictions are restored again. To be recognised in Heaven, our spiritual body must have a recognisable form. Our spiritual body is housed within our earthly body and forms a part of our spirit. Our spirit also contains our memory. At the time of passing, this spiritual body re-creates its earthly human form to provide a vessel in which our spirit travels to Heaven. It is in this form that our spirit energy resides until our spirit unifies and settles in the new spiritual surroundings of Heaven. In Heaven our spiritual body will slowly transform. The physical replica is often the body that is used by spirit when it creates great energy to show itself to you, or to a loved one here on earth. The energy it creates is often seen by people when they describe seeing a ghost, the energy used often affects the temperature of the place where it is seen and people recall this fact. The psychical replica is used by the spirit on occasions when linking with a medium, so that the medium may describe the communicator accurately to the recipient. It is a useful tool with which the medium can provide evidence of existence of survival of the human spirit. So, to begin with in Heaven, we look as we choose to look, that is until our spiritual pathway unfolds and our spiritual progression continues. No need for make-up, hairdressers or weight watchers!

What do they do in Heaven?
Contrary to popular belief, when a spirit passes from this life to Heaven, the new arrival is not issued with a harp, a pair of wings, or a big white,

Keith Charles

fluffy cloud to sit on. If you have the notion or belief that Heaven is a kind of Utopia, think again. Heaven is an interesting and wonderful place. The new spirit might choose to nurse and care for babies and young children who pass over, assist new arrivals in general, or work with animals. The new arrival may choose to devote time in developing creative skills, extending knowledge or increase understanding of humanity. Each and any of the educational activities are available from the great masters and spiritual guides. There are great teachers and orators, wonderful gardens to visit, interesting people to meet. A friend of mine said he would love to have a conversation with Mozart or Churchill. In Heaven he could well get his chance.

Do babies and children grow up in Heaven?
The fact that our spirit has left our body at a young age, or older age for that matter, does not prevent our spiritual growth and progression. Yes, babies and children do grow up in Heaven. But I do not want to alarm parents who ask: 'If my baby grows up, how will I recognise him when I go to Heaven?' The answer is that he will recognise you. Your child will be cared for by a departed member of the family known to it. There is much there in the spirit world for a child to do and experience so its growth in every way is quite normal. One special advantage that

applies to a child as much as it does to any loved one in Heaven is that it may choose to 'look in' on you from its celestial home at any time. In this way, your child is able to watch and chart your earthly life and progress, share in your own experiences of life, in your earthly life. The child will see you go through the ageing process and will recognise you at each stage.

Working with international psychic artist Coral Polge at a meeting in Tolworth, Surrey, she began to draw the face of a young spirit boy who appeared to her. He was about 13. He was a rather sweet-looking boy, quite angelic in appearance, with neatly cropped hair. I was able to link with him and he told me his name was Lawrence. He said he had passed into Heaven when he drowned, and that he wished to link with his mother who had never come to terms with his passing. He told me he had sisters on the earth plane, and that one sister was at the time away from home and that the other had been born since his passing. He knew his mother was not in the audience, but Lawrence directed me to a family in the hall who knew his mother. When I told the family this, they said they were very sorry but they did not know of Lawrence or his mother.

'Yes, they do,' insisted Lawrence. 'They have just moved into their new home and my mother is their new neighbour.'

The family confirmed they had just moved

into a new house a few weeks before. Lawrence knew. He told me that sometimes they had seen the young girl — his sister — take her dog out for a walk. They agreed that they had.

Lawrence asked that his mother be reassured that he was alive and well in the spirit world, and that she should not mourn his loss any more. They would meet again. At the end of the evening, Coral persuaded the family to take her picture of Lawrence and show it to their new neighbour to see if she could, in fact, identify it. Coral rang me a few weeks later to say that the people who had been at this meeting had shown the picture to their neighbour. The woman was told nothing of the circumstances in which it had been drawn, but as the picture was unfolded, the neighbour said, 'My God, that is my Lawrence who drowned several years ago when he was only 13.' The message from Lawrence was passed on to her.

Do people who commit suicide go to Heaven?
Yes, they do. In Heaven they will continue with their spiritual lifetime and pathway and there they will be educated in the ways of making amends for the taking of their own life. Our spiritual guides and masters teach that each person is responsible for his or her own actions. But those who mistakenly believe that suicide is the easy option, a way out of earthly situations and difficulties, which will automatically take them

into God's garden of Heaven and into a spiritual life of bliss, will be very disappointed. These spirits will spend more time in the company of spiritual teachers, learning the lessons they clearly did not learn on earth.

Do disabilities exclude us from Heaven?

I was at a show in Maidstone, Kent, when a very happy spirit communicated with me. He showed himself to me dressed in a sailor's uniform and he appeared to be dancing the hornpipe. This sailor told me his name was Ernie, and then directed me to a man and his wife seated towards the middle of the theatre. Ernie told me they would answer to the name 'Field'. Sure enough, I found Mr and Mrs Field.

Mr Field told me that his grandfather was named Ernest and that he had served in the Royal Navy. Ernie said he had passed to Heaven in the late Seventies, and this was confirmed by Mr Field along with other information I passed on. But I was puzzled that Ernie seemed to be trying to impress me with his dancing skills. At one point I had to tell Mr Field that Ernest was now lifting his trousers, and showing me his legs.

'I understand why he's doing that,' said Mr Field. 'Ernie loved to dance, it was his passion, but later in his life he was involved in an accident at sea, and had both legs amputated. He has obviously got them back again!'

Is there a separate animal Heaven?
No, there is not. Animals, too, have a spirit which continues after their physical death. This spirit also ascends into Heaven. Expressions such as the 'animal kingdom' applies as much in Heaven as it does on earth. Some people who pass over choose to look after the spiritual animals and get much pleasure from doing this. On many occasions, spirit animals have shown themselves to me so that they, too, can give evidence of survival. The animal usually accompanies a human spirit communicator.

Is there a Hell?
The concept of Hell has been created by orthodox religions and is spoken about in the Bible. Unfortunately, some people have been indoctrinated into accepting everything that is written in the Bible is fact. If this is your perception, then what follows will not sit comfortably with you.

There is no Hell. Orthodox religion has created the concept of Hell as a fear factor, to control its followers.

I have been instructed by my spiritual teachers and guides that Hell does not exist. Our spiritual progression takes us all to Heaven and it is there in Heaven where we will each answer for our actions, good or bad, here on earth. Each of us is responsible for our own

Psychic Detective

actions and must be prepared to accept praise or
admonishment for them on our day of spiritual
reckoning.

So-called 'horrible people' will be confined to
strict and intensive spiritual admonishment and
teachings. They are not permitted to receive all
the niceties of spiritual Heaven, with all this has
to offer, until they have worked through their
spiritual karma and have acknowledged the sins
they have committed here on earth.

Is there a time span before someone may communicate?
There is no time span, nor time barrier preventing
a loved one who has passed communicating
through a medium. People tend to feel that
depending on the circumstances of the passing, a
spirit needs recovery time before it may
communicate with its loved ones on earth. It
entirely depends on the spirit of the person
passing; if the desire is strong and the acceptance
immediate, that spirit may well choose to
communicate quickly.

I was taking a show at the Assembly Rooms, in
Tunbridge Wells, Kent, and in the audience I was
aware of four young people sitting in the front
row, a little scruffily dressed, not prepared, as it
were, for an evening out. I estimated their ages to
be between 19 and 23. As the show unfolded, I
was contacted by a young man from Heaven who
told me his name was Jason, who said he wished

to link with the young female in the group of four. Jason described himself to me and said he had been killed in a motorcycle accident. I linked with the young lady and told her of Jason's presence, and passed on his information as he gave it to me. Jason said he had spoken to the young girl on the telephone shortly before he died in the accident. The precise time he gave me was 11.30am. At this, the young girl burst into tears and began to tremble.

Her friends comforted her and when she recovered her composure, she explained to me and the audience that her best friend Jason had been killed on his motorcycle at 11.30am that same morning! She said that she and her friends were on their way home from the hospital when they noticed my evening of clairvoyance. On impulse, they decided to join the audience. So Jason had communicated within a matter of hours of passing from this life!

If the person who died did not believe in life after death, can they still 'come through'?
The fact that a person who has passed over did not believe in life after death makes absolutely no difference to their ability to communicate with their loved ones they have left behind. The non-belief expressed by the individual on earth to their family or friends is purely an opinion they formulated from facts known to them on earth.

Once they arrive in Heaven, they then know there is life after death!

I do not believe in life after death. Can I still receive a message from a loved one who has passed away?
Any person may receive a communication from a loved one who has passed into the higher realms of life, no matter what his religious belief or non-belief. The fact that there is a life after death and the strong desire by the loved one in Heaven who wishes to get through to them and communicate, will not prevent a message being passed on either directly or indirectly by a third person.

How do I stop feeling guilty?
This is another question I am often asked for varying reasons. People tell me they feel guilty because they had an argument, or disagreement, with their loved one before that person passed away. They said words which they did not really mean, and which they now regretted. Guilt may be felt by some, believing they should have done, or could have done, more to help a loved one. Others feel guilty because a family member has committed suicide and the surviving relatives or friends feel guilty that they were unaware of the pain, problems and anguish their loved one had been experiencing. Guilt is an emotion, as is love. I believe that the only people who feel guilty are those who really care, the individual who is honest

with himself, who believes, rightly or wrongly, that he could and should have made a difference.

So the way to stop feeling guilty is to dismiss that feeling within. Say a little mental prayer to your loved one, a quick 'sorry' and let that be the end of your guilt feeling. Sometimes that feeling of guilt can go on for years and just eat away at you, but spirit can go to extraordinary lengths to redress the balance.

Is there any spiritual jealousy?
There is no spiritual jealousy in Heaven. Jealousy is a physical emotion created by experiences gained on earth. I am instructed by Tobias that jealousy simply does not exist in spirit and any emotions linked to jealousy are forgotten and dismissed once the loved one passes into Heaven. Where there may have been more than one partner on earth, love overrides any jealousy which may have been created on earth.

In 1981, I was conducting a meeting in Berkshire when I received a message for a lady seated in the centre of the church. All had been going well up to this point.

'Madam, I have your husband here with me,' I told the lady.

'Which one?' she asked.

I wasn't all that experienced at the time so her response threw me a little. I returned to the spirit communicator and asked, 'Please tell me your name so that I can tell her which husband you were.'

He simply said he was her first husband.

'So, who is it?' the lady called out.

I had no option but just to give what he was telling me. 'Madam, he says to tell you, it is your first husband,' was my reply.

The lady thought for a moment, then said, 'You can keep him then. He was no good to me when he was here and he is no good to me now!'

I was very surprised by this reaction and I didn't really know whether to laugh or to cry!

Is there reincarnation?
Reincarnation is the return of a spiritual life from Heaven back to an earthly life. Life on earth is not the inception of spirit. We are spirit before we come to earth. Reincarnation is not an automatic right, nor does it occur for everyone. Do people die, go to Heaven and then return to human form again immediately? The teachings that I have received from my spiritual guide, Tobias, reveals that there is reincarnation for some. Reincarnation may be a necessity for some in order that they may return to earth to learn a lesson, or lessons, they failed to learn in their first earthly life.

It would be extremely naïve and selfish to think, or suppose, that we are the only level of intelligent existence. To continue our spiritual pathway, reincarnation to earth may be necessary. Our spiritual education is continuous and should our spiritual master consider it a requirement for our spiritual progression to be enhanced by a return to earth and human form, then we will be reincarnated. I would imagine that if and when reincarnation is necessary, it is highly unlikely that a child would be reborn to the same parents.

Joanna Lumley, the famous British actress, told the *Daily Mail* in an interview, 'I don't believe you can help being reincarnated, whether you believe in it or not. You're going to be recycled, let's put it like that, in some way. Whether I will come back as me, Joanna Lumley, into the spirit of a something or other, I'm not sure, but I certainly can remember things that have never happened to me, places I've been to, this *déjà vu* thing, or the sudden closeness you feel to people you don't know.'

What is spiritual healing?
Some people use the term 'faith healing'. Spiritual healing does not require the 'patient' to have any faith in order for the mechanics of spiritual healing to work. Healing may be administered either by contact healing or absent healing, when prayers are offered for the individual's physical and spiritual well-being. Healing is a natural quality within each of us. In healing, the healer links in with his

own spiritual guides and helpers in order to tap the great spiritual energy that helps the patient.

Are psychic surgeons genuine?
Psychic surgeons are involved in spiritual healing, but whereas the spiritual healer may work alongside his spiritual guides, psychic surgeons often work in trance, alongside their spiritual guide. There has been great controversy involving Philippino psychic surgeons, although I have heard from some friends that they have received great benefit from visiting British psychic surgeons.

What is an aura?
We know that we have a physical body which houses our spirit. Some people who are sensitive and particularly well trained as mediums may see and tune into the protective energy which naturally protects us. The protective energy which surrounds our body is known as the aura. It has a shape, is vibrant and has colour. It is a form of spiritual light which contains information about the individual it envelops, information which a medium is able to 'read'. If you have seen a halo painted over a Saint, then some say this is the artist being made aware of the aura. Depending on the configuration, colour, shape and strength of the aura, the medium may well be able to give quite an accurate reading about

what makes that person tick.

Many people can pick up another person's aura. It may be that the first time you meet someone you accidentally tap into their aura and you seem remarkably aware of something about that person before they even speak to you. Such as that they feel unwell, or have personal problems. It may work the other way, and you feel very wary of someone. The aura may be made up of one or several colours or shades of colour and each may reveal information about the individual. It may be that there is one strong, prevalent colour which the medium may be able to interpret as some kind of stress — or something else.

What is ectoplasm?
Not many mediums around today can claim to produce ectoplasm. It is a term used to describe a substance produced by a medium in trance. It may be produced by those sitting in a physical 'circle' by a physical medium. Ectoplasm is emitted from the medium and it may look like smoke, or even something more dense than smoke. Although I have never experienced this phenomenon, I have spoken to older mediums and spiritualists who have produced, or have experienced, the production of this substance. I understand that photographs have been taken in genuine cases of ectoplasm production. It is claimed that the ectoplasm can form into a shape

representing the form and physical shape of a loved one who has passed over to enable them to communicate with loved ones on earth.

Is 'divining' or 'divination' a spiritual gift?

I believe there is no evidence to suggest that a person who has the ability to divine, using rods or sticks to seek out or pinpoint water sources, or even oil, needs to be a medium. Occasionally, people such as Uri Geller claim to have used their psychic gift and powers in this way when searching for sources of oil. Divining rods, usually V-shaped, or two separate rods, are now man-made, although I understand original rods were cut from hazelwood, or even two crude twigs. Some diviners claim to have psychic ability and this may be true, but I have yet to meet a diviner who claims to be a medium. At the same time, I know people with psychic abilities who have tried divining with some success.

Can I meet my departed loved ones in my dreams?

I frequently meet people who say they meet up with departed loved ones in their dreams. These experiences are often happy and uplifting. They may be involved in an activity they shared, a familiar place they visited, or simply a heart-to-heart conversation. To the dreamer these are utterly convincing. My spirit guide, Tobias, explains that during our sleeping period, there comes a time when our earthly bodies are closest to death. At this time our etheric body is able to leave our physical body and journey to the spirit world. This happens deep within our subconscious mind. In the spirit world, we meet up with and join our loved ones who may have recently passed, or those we loved, who passed many years ago. There are those who constantly dream, some who 'astral travel', and those who are still waiting for such an experience. Where there is an existing bond of love that cannot be broken by death and a strong desire to communicate, this state of meeting in dreams is one convenient way in which communication is possible.

What are earthbound spirits?
Some spirits are earthbound in the sense that sometimes due to the traumatic circumstances of their passing, or through their own non-acceptance of death, or even through their own desire, they choose to stay close to the scene of their passing. A spirit may want to stay close to its loved ones, or even to its workplace here on earth. This is a very rare occurrence and the earthbound spirit may be easily helped on its way to Heaven by an experienced medium, or by simple prayer.

What is meant by a spirit 'guide'?

Spirit guides, or helpers as they are sometimes called, are those spirit beings who have themselves been trained and educated in Heaven to accompany us in this earthly life. Most people may be familiar with the non-spiritualist expression 'guardian angel'. We all have a particular guardian angel, but we have more than one spirit guide. Our guides do not necessarily all do the same job for us. Often people question why so many North American Indians appear as healing guides. I have heard it said it is due to the lifestyle they led on this earth and the fact that they were very spiritual and very reliant on nature to assist in their healing remedies. For similar reasons, Chinese guides are often philosophers. But whatever the nationality or nature of the guide, they have one purpose and that is to help us in our spiritual development.

We also have one especially important guide, or spiritual helper, who is our 'door keeper'. He is responsible for acting as a spiritual 'bouncer' or bodyguard, and is the 'master of ceremonies' who allows and facilitates communicators and guides to link with the medium. The door keeper is responsible for giving spiritual protection to the medium. My own door keeper is Kurinda and I have seen him on several occasions.

Keith Charles

Is the ouija board dangerous?

Curiosity is probably the most common reason why people experiment with a ouija board. This instrument, or an adaptation of it, was used quite frequently in Victorian times as a form of amusement or as a parlour game. But this is not its proper use and there is a much more serious side to its correct usage. I have been present when a ouija board has been used on three or four occasions. At such times it was in the presence of a church minister, or in the company of other mediums. These meetings were opened with prayer.

The ouija board is less demanding on spiritual energy. For instance, if five mediums are sitting together using a ouija board, each using only 50 per cent of their energy, then there is a pooled use of 250 per cent of the energy of those at the sitting — a very powerful tool. When used by mediums, the ouija board is a useful link to the spirit world, and is used to seek the truth about the spirit world. It is a powerful way to 'talk' to spirit communicators, to ask them for their fullest and most personal details, along with their new world surroundings. I have heard it said that such eminent people as Sir Arthur Conan Doyle and Sir Winston Churchill both used and communicated through the ouija board.

But be warned — the ouija board should not be misused. It should not be used by the inexperienced as a game or a joke. Think of the ouija board as a precious instrument that you would not allow into the hands of an inexperienced user. In the hands of the wrong users, a tenuous link might be made with spirit and messages received misinterpreted. I have not had much worthwhile evidence from a ouija board and it is not a favourite of mine.

What are poltergeists?

Poltergeist, from the German '*poltern*' which means 'to make noises' and '*geist*', German for 'ghost'. So a poltergeist is literally 'a noisy ghost'. Such noisy ghosts are usually earthbound spirits. They have been known to cause things to move, doors to slam, temperature changes and sometimes property to be broken. Houses where such activity takes place would be considered haunted, and it could be that the occupier in residence may be gifted or sensitive, even to the point of having seen the 'ghost' responsible.

It should be said that most alleged poltergeist activity is not sinister or evil, but is created by a spiritual being or loved one attempting to make its presence known, to reassure those on earth that it is 'alive and well' in Heaven.

Is there sex in the afterlife?

One of the more frequently asked questions by both men and women, and there's nothing strange in wondering if there is sex there, any more than it might be to wonder if we need food in Heaven, or can play football! I feel it appropriate to relate the events of a 'haunting' I was called in to investigate in 1997.

A respectable middle-class woman living in a Victorian house in a pretty Sussex village with her husband and family came to me in considerable distress. She told me the house was basically a very happy family home with a lovely 'feel' to it but, again, the lady I will call Mrs P, had many experiences of the presence of a spirit in her bedroom. She told me that usually these visits took place around dawn, when her husband and family were away and she was alone in bed. She told me how she would hear footsteps, as though someone was walking upstairs and entering her bedroom. To begin with, this was all that would happen. But as time went by, she'd hear the footsteps come into the bedroom and distinctly feel someone lie down on the bed beside her. She tried leaving her bedside lamp on, but this didn't deter the presence from coming to her bed and lying down. Then one morning she said she woke from her sleep, stretched out an arm, and touched the hand of the spirit, which frightened her. Mrs P further explained that sometimes the spirit made sexual advances to her, at which times she experienced strong feelings of intimacy.

Probably like you, I wondered why she didn't

simply move, or get up! Mrs P explained that being half asleep and almost paralysed with fear, she was unable to move or even to speak. In fact, such things are not particularly uncommon, but Mrs P was extremely angry and disgusted that she should be subjected to these kind of advances from a spirit.

When I visited the house, I was immediately aware of the presence of two spirits within this peaceful home. One was a woman who had passed over about 80 years ago, but she was not responsible for Mrs P's problems. The other spirit was that of a man who made himself known to me as Bill. I was able to communicate with him. Bill was a young man in his early twenties. He had a bold personality which made it easy for him to tell me how he had been killed in enemy action in the First World War. Bill said he was visiting the house to look for his girlfriend who had lived there at the time of his death, but found Mrs P who bore a remarkable resemblance to this girlfriend even though she was older. It was clear that he had chosen to become earthbound because of the tragic circumstances of his passing, and he would not accept that he had died. I was able to help him with his onward journey to Heaven. Mrs P has not been troubled since.

What are tarot cards?
I put tarot cards, runes, palmistry and crystal balls

all in the same category. They are all manufactured items to assist the 'reader' who has developed a psychic gift to channel and concentrate this gift to a central focal point so that readings can be given. Tarot cards use symbols and pictures as keys to a reading, and although the precise origin of these cards cannot be established, it is thought that they may have been an ancient Egyptian gift. The tarot cannot possibly form a link with the spirit world so I do not use them. I put the tarot and other 'fringe' tools on a par with psychometry. A good medium does not need them.

What is regression?
Hypnotherapy regression is the means by which people may explore past lives. Those of us trained and experienced in regression have no problem tapping into past lives which are contained within the spiritual memory held by each of us. In research into hypnotherapy, I have experienced regression and examined the work of hypnotherapists and regressionists.

Owen Potts, a psychic friend of mine, is an experienced regressionist and I took up an offer by him to go to his Thames-side, London office to explore my own past lives. During my regression I was taken back to when I was a Confederate soldier at the time of the American Civil War. I saw myself in a Confederate uniform, with other soldiers. We had been retreating, and a small group of about 30 of us had been cut off from the main troop in a small woodland copse. I was hiding behind a fallen tree. A cavalry officer was leading a charge and as he attacked our position, he ran me through with his sword. It was not a pleasant death, but whilst in regression I felt no pain either physically or emotionally.

Having completed my regression, I opened my eyes and I was astonished to find that this process had taken nearly one hour, yet had seemed like only a few minutes to me. My advice to anyone interested in exploring their own past lives is to do so only with a fully qualified regressionist. It does not work for everyone.

Conclusion

1 have noticed an upsurge of interest in psychic phenomena and the paranormal. And there seems to be a change of attitude toward the question 'Is there life after death?' People generally are becoming more aware of their own spirituality and desire to get in tune with their own psychic gifts. They are beginning to question old attitudes toward religion. Individuals are aware of the significance of their psychic and intuitive abilities and wish to channel them to a more useful and positive purpose, and the increased interest in alternative medicine, spiritual healing and development is ever-growing. The fact that orthodox Chrisitanity is training people to communicate with 'spirits' in what they term 'exorcisms' is further recognition of the communion of spirits. I would love to see the day when the orthodox religions make use of mediums (something I am sure will eventually happen) in order to unite and help all mankind

understand the purpose of life both materially and spiritually.

As for my own aspirations? I will continue to demonstrate my spiritual gifts at theatres, so giving a shop window to spiritualism and mediumship to those who wish to 'dip their toe in the water.'

I will continue to help police forces and investigators throughout the world when called upon, hopefully providing help and assistance where traditional policing methods have proved fruitless. I am sure that the prejudices held by some can only be overturned by good psychic exponents. We live in a world of change, rapid change, and I am convinced it will not be long before police forces will feel rather less embarrassed or inhibited about making more use of genuine psychics and mediums. We all want a good world in which to live and raise our families. I hope that I contribute positively. I know that if I help just one person each day, then I am doing my bit.

Now you are in a position to make up your own mind ...